Cheers and Amen

A year-long, 50-state adventure

Dean and Mindy Anderson

ISBN-10:1720996857
ISBN-13:9781720996859

Dedicated to our parents,
our children,
and everyone else who made this adventure possible.

CONTENTS

Acknowledgements

INTRODUCTION

December 30, 2015

We were on the 580, driving through the Altamont Pass east of Oakland, looking at the windmills. Even though I was driving, I could look at them because we were only going fifteen miles an hour. I couldn't ever remember traffic being any worse in the Bay Area. It was nearly 6:00 pm on Wednesday, and I figured most of these people were heading home. Some of them would be going to work the next day, but many had a long holiday weekend ahead of them, maybe even a vacation.

We weren't going on vacation, exactly. We certainly weren't going home, because we didn't have a home anymore. One of our daughters called us "optionally homeless." We planned to spend the next year, 2016, on the road, visiting at least one church and one bar in every state.

The idea had come to us a decade before, when I was working full time as a hotel night auditor and part-time at a church and writing a children's mystery series on the side. Years earlier, we'd come up with the idea of writing a book about visiting a church in every state, and we'd pitched it at a writers conference. Shockingly, nobody leaped at giving a couple of amateurs a $50,000 advance to create a coffee table book. So we kept our day jobs and our little rented house in Healdsburg.

On occasion, we wondered about churches in other parts of the country. How was a Baptist church in Mississippi different from a Lutheran church in, say, North Dakota? Were people in city churches looking for different things than those in the suburbs? Who preferred house churches, and who liked megachurches? Why did people make such a big deal over music and buildings? Did people care more about preaching or fellowship?

Almost ten years later, we found ourselves reconsidering the book idea. Jil, our youngest, graduated from college but had stayed in New York; our middle child, Paige was married; and our oldest, Bret, was on his own. That stage of parenting was complete, and we were suddenly released from several time and financial obligations.

A second significant change was my mother's death. After my dad died, we'd gotten into the habit of going to Mom's house for dinner most Sunday nights. Along with my sister and other family members, we helped out with doctor's appointments and other errands. Though we missed her dearly after she passed away, we found ourselves with a certain freedom. She'd left some money to each of her children and their families, and suddenly the trip seemed possible.

We realized the focus of our adventure would be very different from what we had first imagined. In the original version, we'd anticipated keeping our day jobs and our little rental house in Healdsburg and traveling -- usually by plane -- to different states each weekend. Now that we had a little money saved and no children at home, experiencing the country in a giant, year-long road trip seemed like a more practical (if unusual) plan. We'd have one week for every state, plus Washington, D.C. We'd even have a week to spare.

To test the process, we decided to visit and blog about churches throughout California during 2015. In January we headed to the farthest north, south, east, and west California churches we could find, driving up to 24 hours over each two-day weekend. Other months we followed themes such as "churches used in movies" and "churches attended by writers we like." We spent a great deal of time in the car together that year, and we enjoyed it. We posted about a different church every week. We even got business cards.

And we put a lot of miles on the minivan. When the guys in the service department noticed we were bringing our trusty 2006 Dodge Caravan in pretty much monthly, they asked about it. We told them, and asked (a little anxiously), "Is this car up for traveling the country next year?" Every time, they answered in the affirmative.

I was working the 11:00 pm to 7:00 am shift at a hotel. Mindy was working at a lumber yard from 2:00 pm to 10:00 pm or so (occasionally as late as 2:00 am). Except for visiting churches, we didn't see each other very much, so we enjoyed those weekends together. A whole year together sounded pretty good. Still, we each wondered about being together all day, every day, for a year.

We also wondered about living with just what fit into the minivan. We began to plan for the trip. How much money would we need? Should we rig up the van as a kind of camper? Would old acquaintances let us stay with them? How would we choose the right church in each state full of churches?

Mindy and I are Christians. We believe Jesus is the only begotten Son of God, the Savior of the world. When people asked, "Will you be going to mosques and synagogues and temples as well as churches?" we answered, "Nope."

We tried to explain that we wanted to write about what we know, and we know churches. More importantly, we believe that the world needs Jesus. We decided we would go to Protestant or Catholic or Orthodox churches as long as they honored Jesus. We wanted to get a better idea of the health of the Church in the United States, but we also decided to avoid some churches called "Christian" that aren't Christian in our understanding of the term.

When we started to tell people about visiting a church in every state, people in churches tended to respond with an interested, "Huh!" People who didn't go to church responded with a quite different, "Huh" and the conversation usually ended right there. We had a feeling the project might need something more.

It was likely more than a few itinerant preachers had gone to churches in every state, and probably some had done it within a year. I got to thinking about what kind of places would be everywhere we went. We talked about what kind of places we could meet people and talk. We thought of bars.

I'd worked for years in hotels with bars, but rarely went to one otherwise. As far as she could remember, Mindy had never sat at a bar, so we figured our learning experience might make for interesting reading. We figured that like churches, bars could be found in most communities. It seemed unlikely there'd been many people who had been to a church and a bar in every state, especially not in a single year.

Suddenly, people were much more interested. Probably the best reaction came from a complete stranger, a hostess at an Italian restaurant in San Francisco. We were walking down the street, and she gave us a card for her restaurant. So we gave her a card for our blogs and told her our plan to visit a church and bar in every state. She was quiet for a moment, then exclaimed, "F--- YEAH!" As we walked away, Mindy murmured, "I think we might be onto something."

For weeks, we'd been getting rid of stuff. We sold some things. Our son took some furniture for his apartment. Eighteen stuffed storage bins went to stay with Sonoma County friends and family for the year. We packed our van so full that we could only look back using the side mirrors. We made trip after trip to Goodwill and Salvation Army. The morning of December 30, we were still cleaning and getting rid of things. We made a last-minute call to 1-800-GOT-JUNK for stuff the Salvation Army didn't want and the apartment dumpster wouldn't take. It was afternoon before we handed our keys over to the apartment manager, and we still had to make a stop to get rid of the cable box. (It was not a quick in and out at Comcast because it never is.)

But not a lot of progress was being made that Wednesday evening. We'd hoped to leave early in the morning, drive all day and spend the night in a cabin at Calico Ghost Town in San Bernardino County.

Somewhere on the Richmond Bridge, with traffic slowed so much we could look across the bay at San Francisco's skyscrapers and the Golden Gate Bridge, we decided to cancel our reservations at Calico Ghost Town. That meant we'd forfeit the forty dollars or so we'd paid for that night's stay.

"Are we going to be losing deposit money the rest of the trip?" I asked Mindy. "Let's not make any more reservations."

"We have a reservation for the next four nights at a Best Western in Las Vegas."

"Okay, then. None after that."

We finally made it over the Altamont Pass and started moving south at dizzying speeds of forty to fifty miles an hour. We made it to the I-5, the central freeway which divides the east and west in California. Usually, people treat I-5 like it's the Autobahn, but even it was having a slow day.

Around 7:00, we pulled off at Santa Nella and ate our first meal of the trip at a Popeye's Louisiana Kitchen. Neither of us had ever been to the chicken chain, but we thought it was funny that we'd be in Louisiana in just a few more weeks. After dinner, we thought about hitting the road again but checked into a Motel 6 instead, paying extra for horrible WiFi. The first 150 or so miles of our big trip had taken over five hours, and we were already tired.

The next afternoon, we crossed into Nevada at precisely 3:00 pm on New Year's Eve Day - our first state, we hoped, of fifty.

Of course, many trips end ugly in Las Vegas, what with the gambling, the drinking, and time spent with prostitutes. We only did two of those things, though. The last two.

1
COOKIES AND HOPE

"Would you like some homemade cookies?" I asked the woman. She was quite obviously homeless, with blonde, grey, unkempt hair, and well-worn clothes. She was also stoned and probably a bit mad.

"You can take those cookies," she answered, "And stick them…" Well, I won't complete her sentence. It's enough to say that I'd rather eat the cookies, a mix of chocolate chip and peanut butter. She continued to yell and swear, and it seemed best to keep moving down North Las Vegas Blvd.

We were in a section of Las Vegas that seemed a world away from the Las Vegas we'd experienced when we arrived on New Year's Eve. The tourism board would prefer people to see the excitement at the other end of the Strip rather than what Kathleen Quirk was about to show us.

Initially, a friend of a friend had invited us to stay in Las Vegas with her family, but the dates didn't work out, so I Googled away and came across an article in the Las Vegas Review-Journal about a woman who baked cookies and gave them to street people. I found Kathleen on Facebook and asked if she would take us on a cookie run. She agreed to take us out the Saturday after New Years. Before that, though, we needed to get settled in Sin City and experience New Year's Eve Las Vegas style.

***

Free buses to and from the Strip were available during the afternoon and evening (driving in Las Vegas on New Year's Eve didn't seem smart -- and anyway, cars weren't allowed in much of the area that night). We wandered in and out of casinos looking for the oddest pop culture reference on a slot machine (Airplane!, Willy Wonka, Gremlins, or Beetlejuice?)

If we had expected to find churches on the Strip, we'd have been disappointed. We saw plenty of wedding chapels, but not what we were looking for. Most of the chapels were closed that evening, anyway.

Bars, however, were abundant and busy. By 9:00 pm, a whole lot of tipsy people were mingling with the families walking the crowded streets. We were on the tired side, so we headed back to the hotel. We sorted through some belongings and watched a few fireworks from our windows at midnight.

***

We weren't sure how to spend the first day of 2016. Watching Bowl games didn't have much appeal, so we decided to go to the movies.

We already had two things we planned to do in every state (the bar and the church); we decided to add a third for our own entertainment. I guess we could have gone bowling in every state, gone antiquing in every state, or played putt-putt golf in every state. We like those okay, but did we like them enough to dedicate our somewhat limited time and very limited money to them?

We love movies though. And movie theaters. Moviegoing was something we'd done with our parents when we were kids and with our kids when we were parents.

So we went to the movies. We decided to see *The Big Short*, a film about the financial meltdown of 2008. As we went into The Brenden Palms Casino, we were both wondering if adding "going to the movies in every state" was a wise financial move on our part. We had about 30,000 in the bank -- almost enough to cover our trip, we hoped, if we scrimped and saved every way we could. We anticipated a little income from tax refunds, writing, and a quarterly check from my mom's estate. We were also trusting that the minivan wouldn't break down.

Suddenly, in the middle of the movie (which quite reasonably focused on Wall Street, New York, and Washington D.C.), there was an extended sequence in Las Vegas.

You might think we're silly, but it seemed like that sequence was God saying, "Hey, this movie in every state thing? I'm okay with it."

There were a couple of other things we decided to do in every state. In addition to the bar and church -- and a movie in a theater -- we decided to watch (another) movie that was set or filmed in that state. We brought many of those films on DVDs in the van with us, and some we streamed. Our first such film was *Lost in America*, which was a pretty perfect start for the trip. It's about a husband and wife (Albert Brooks and Julie Hagerty) who decide to chuck it all and go off in a Winnebago to find America. (Spoiler, our trip went better than theirs.) For awhile, Mindy used #lostinamerica on her instagram posts.

We also committed to watching a TV show set or filmed in each state. I reported back every week via Twitter to a podcast called "TV Talk Machine" hosted by Tim Goodman of the Hollywood Reporter. And every week, his co-host, Jason Snell, would report which state "Dean of the 707" (my phone's area code) was in and what TV show we watched. (The first was a *Crime Story* episode set in Las Vegas).

***

That night, January 1, we went to our first bar.

I didn't feel we had a choice about visiting this particular bar. Years ago I worked at the Hotel Healdsburg, which had a restaurant, the Dry Creek Kitchen. Chef Charlie Palmer is one of the owners of the hotel and the Chef and owner of the DCK. He was a good boss and a good guy, so it seemed like we should take the opportunity to visit one of his other properties for our bar visit.

We might have gone to Aureole at Mandalay Bay even if it weren't for Charlie because it had a four-story wine tower as its central feature. I'd seen it featured years before when our daughters were hooked on Samantha Brown's Travel Channel shows.

After asking several people in Mandalay Bay for directions to Aureole (severely mangling the pronunciation), we made our way to the reception desk, where we asked how to get to the Lounge. The hostess told us to go down the staircase which circled the Wine Tower.

We realized we were underdressed. Mindy was wearing a casual dress and I was in black jeans and a short-sleeved button-front shirt, but bartenders and the male guests wore coat and tie. The women were wearing high heels and clothes to go with them. It was the first of many times we'd feel out of place walking into a bar.

I should probably describe Mindy and me. We were both 54 years old, and so we were rarely asked for I.D. I'm 6'3," and Mindy is 5'2" (when we kissed at our wedding, people giggled at my need to lean down). Both of us look more like the before rather than the after photo for a diet plan.

At some bars, we figured we'd be out of place because everyone was much younger. There were places where we were better dressed than anyone else (as frightening as that is to contemplate.) More often, we felt out of place as the only strangers in the bar.

At Aureole, only a few people were at the bar in the lounge. One couple didn't seem interested in anyone else in the world, and we found seats at the end of the bar nearest the restaurant area, and the bartender handed us a tablet with the drinks menu, showing us how to swipe the screen to turn the pages. We overheard another guest request a paper menu, but we were impressed by the technology.

As we scrolled through the by-the-glass wine list, we felt the hometown spirit when we saw the Sonoma County vineyards and wineries featured along with European labels. Still, we decided to start the year with cocktails. The Chocolate Martini looked amazing, and since we'd already eaten dinner, I thought it sounded like a suitable dessert. It's not exactly what you'd call a manly drink, but it was delicious. Mindy went with a Raspberry Lemon Drop.

Both the cocktails and the menu made us wonder how the bars in the weeks ahead would compare, and we didn't really have the background to make a guess. We were pretty sure most other bars we'd visit would have cheaper drinks, and Mindy hoped they'd have menus.

We knew we needed to talk to people, but we were nervous about approaching strangers in a bar. On that first night, we decided the bartenders weren't too intimidating.

Sal had taken our order and mixed our drinks. For the first time, we asked the two questions we planned to ask at bars for the rest of the year, "What makes for a good bar?" and "What makes for a good church?"

Sal was quick to answer what made for a good bar. "Good bartenders. The ingredients for drinks are pretty much the same everywhere. The bartender makes the difference." A good church, Sal said, had a good pastor.

We didn't realize it until we'd been to a few more bars in a few more states, but bartenders tended to say a bartender makes the bar. They often followed that by saying pastors make the church.

When we asked for a good story, he told us something that had happened during his first year at Aureole.

A man planned to propose to his girlfriend and asked Sal to find him roses, which Sal managed to do, even though it was after 11:00 pm. The man paid generously for the flowers, and at midnight, the man got down on one knee and proposed to his girlfriend. The woman said yes, taking the roses. It was a beautiful moment.

Unfortunately, at that same moment, another woman wearing a short skirt walked by. The man's eye followed her. The new fiancee couldn't help noticing, and she expressed her outrage by hitting the man with roses. Repeatedly. Rose petals and awkward feelings spread throughout the restaurant.

Dave, the other bartender, had been at Aureole for four years, and he'd been tending bar for seventeen years. He said he'd begun by working at a small, family-owned Italian restaurant, then moved on to an Applebee's. He didn't speak badly of the chain, saying they make a good, consistent product, but he said that a chain doesn't give room for self-expression.

I asked Dave what he looked for in a good bar. We heard variations on his answer over the next year as well.

He said it depends on what you're looking for, what kind of environment you're in the mood for. Sometimes, he said, you'd like to be someplace quiet for a well-crafted drink. Sometimes you're in a party mood and want a more festive atmosphere. He was ready to recommend local bars that would match a variety of moods, which we appreciated.

When I asked what would make for a good church, Dave said he couldn't answer that since he was Jewish. So I asked what would make for a good temple. He said it should be a simple place: people, chairs, and a suitable place for the Torah.

We finished our drinks and paid. As Mindy and I walked out, we smiled at each other. We had visited our first bar -- with at least forty nine left to go. The next morning we would visit our first church, more or less.

**

Our new Facebook friend, Kathleen, had invited us to meet her at the Las Vegas Rescue Mission. A few blocks away, we drove by a homeless camp; pup tents and cardboard boxes. Kathleen was waiting for us in the parking lot, and Mindy noticed and admired her knee-high leather boots. She grinned and admitted belonging to a shoe of the month club, then offered us a tour of the grounds.

Residents working through recovery from various addictions are asked to commit to the program for a year. We could only go into the lobbies; the rooms are (understandably) kept private. We saw the program's classrooms, decorated with Scripture, inspirational, and informational posters. We peeked into the computer room, which is available to help residents completing the program look for work.

The Mission had a thrift store, and we were excited to be able to donate some of the stuff we'd already realized wasn't what we needed for a year-long adventure. We'd spent part of New Year's Eve sorting through our clothes and other belongings, and Kathleen helped us get our bags to one of the sorting areas where several workers were happy to ham it up for a photo. Kathleen showed us the dining room and kitchen she supervised, where hundreds of people are fed every day.

When Kathleen had begun baking and distributing cookies, four years earlier, she hadn't been off the streets long. She told us she'd been a prostitute, an addict, and a thief, but then she got to know Jesus, and her life changed.

We drove a few miles to North Las Vegas Boulevard, where Kathleen hoped to offer cookies and hope to people on the street. She carried a black and grey backpack packed with baggies full of home-made cookies, and she had a few $1s and $5s rolled up in her pocket. We hadn't walked far before Kathleen saw a tall, thin man in worn jeans coming unsteadily down the sidewalk between a dilapidated motel and another, equally faded, building. She gave him a hug and a baggie of cookies and chatted with him about people they both knew. After a few minutes, she reached into her pocket and gave the man a $5 bill as they said goodbye.

"I used to party with him," she told us as we walked on. "He hit me in the face once, but I don't think he remembers that."

I asked Kathleen why she gave out money since I'd read that experts said giving cash wasn't helpful to the homeless in the long run. "I know, I know," she said, "But when I lived on the street, I always said I didn't believe in God. Still, when I was hungry, I'd ask God for a dollar for a hot dog. So now I think when I give out money, maybe I'm answering someone's prayer."

I asked Kathleen to tell me her favorite story from handing out cookies. She said, "Oh, I guess that would be the time the man put a gun to my head."

She said she'd met a woman while handing out cookies. After they'd talked a while, Kathleen asked if the woman wanted to get out of the street life. The woman said she was fine, so Kathleen gave her a business card and told the woman to call her if she ever changed her mind.

Not long after that, the woman called and asked Kathleen to get her. When Kathleen knocked on the door, a man opened the door, put a gun to Kathleen's head, and told her to leave his girl alone. She left.

Days later, while driving, Kathleen saw the woman. Kathleen pulled over and said, "If you want out of the life, get in the car now." The woman got in. Kathleen called a man she knew who'd offered to help women who needed to get out of the area. He drove to Las Vegas from Texas and back so the woman could get back to her mother's house.

A couple of years had gone by since the incident, and Kathleen had gotten a phone call from the woman just a few weeks before we met her. The woman told Kathleen that she'd gotten married, had a child, and was doing well -- thanks, in part, to some cookies and hope.

Kathleen told us she'd be speaking at an A.A. meeting at a church that evening and asked us to come. That left our afternoon free to visit some chapels of a different kind.

***

Nevada weddings have long been the stuff of American folklore. Your Chers and Britneys go to Vegas to begin their three-day marriages. Everyone has heard the stories, read the books, or watched the movies about people getting drunk and then married in Vegas (for example, see *The Hangover*. Or don't, depending on your tolerance for Zach Galifianakis).

We were curious whether wedding chapels were considered churches by those who were married there or those who worked in them. The casino wedding chapels had been closed on New Year's Eve when we'd looked (even Las Vegas has limits). Still, we found wedding chapels in some pretty strange places -- the big Harley Davidson store had a space for weddings among the antique motorcycles in their balcony museum.

Hoping to get an answer, I asked the woman at the reception desk in Cupid's Wedding Chapel, "Do people have a choice about whether to have a religious or secular wedding?"

She answered, "Well, we're not a church. We have a variety of people who do services for us that are licensed by the state to perform weddings. They have all kinds of backgrounds."

I took that as a "No."

For some reason, people still choose to have weddings at the "chapels" rather than at the courthouse, which is just a few blocks down the street from where many of the chapels are located. Architecturally, a lot of the chapels look like churches, but they don't have crosses or Bibles. They often have doves, though. Maybe not Holy Spirit doves, but doves.

We saw several drive-through wedding chapels; all seemed to be accessorized with strings of lights -- neon or otherwise -- for that romantic touch. (Later in the year, we visited a couple in Missouri who had taken advantage of this service. Jon, one of my youth group students back in the day, was moving cross-country with his girlfriend, Briana. On a lark, they decided to get married as they drove east. The drive-through chapel was the quickest and cheapest wedding available, but I believe they opted out of the Elvis officiant option.)

My parents, who lived in Los Angeles, couldn't afford a formal wedding, so they decided to get married in Las Vegas, taking my mom's parents along (it was the only vacation my grandfather took in his life). The pastor who officiated their wedding at Wee Kirk o' the Heather (featured years later in the Coen Brothers' film *Intolerable Cruelty*) invited them to come to his church the next day. When they did, he introduced them to his congregation as the first couple who had ever taken him up on his invitation.

You know these Las Vegas marriages don't stick -- Mom and Dad's lasted only 54 years (until they were parted by death).

***

We were a little early getting to the church where the AA meeting was going to be. It was a mid-20th-century building on a residential street a few blocks east of the Strip, and we nodded at the smokers outside as we went through the door into the meeting room. We made name tags for ourselves from the stack at the door and resisted adding "We're Just Visitors" or "We Were Invited" or "We're not Alcoholics." We looked around the room, which reminded Mindy a little of an elementary school auditorium. Various people were greeting Kathleen, so we said hello as well, then went to the back of the room to chat with people coming in. Mindy got into a conversation about our trip with two men who liked coming to this particular AA meeting even though they lived about an hour away in Arizona. One of them was particularly excited; he and his wife had walked across the United States. The room was noisy and the meeting was about to begin, but he made it clear that God had taken care of them and that he was sure God would take care of us as well.

As the meeting opened, people were invited to share their stories. One dark-haired young man who seemed to be in his late teens talked about how he had only recently stopped drinking and using, and it was really hard but really worthwhile. Some people shared awful stories of things they had done in their lives: vehicular disasters, neglecting pets, stealing from parents. As the speakers described their horrible stories, others laughed -- not in derision, but because they could relate.

After a break, Kathleen came forward to share her story. She grew up in an abusive home in New Jersey and began drinking and getting in trouble at an early age. Eventually, a New Jersey judge said she wouldn't have to go to prison if she left the state. Kathleen flew to Las Vegas resolved to change her life. That resolution lasted about four hours after arriving in Nevada, and for two decades she lived what she admits was a fairly debauched life. While working as a prostitute, she realized she could steal from the Johns without needing to turn a trick (they were unlikely to call the police, since prostitution, legal in other parts of Nevada, isn't legal in Las Vegas). She stole even from those who were kind and tried to help her, but eventually, it all became too much. She trusted her life to the God whose existence she had denied.

The meeting closed with the Lord's Prayer -- which may be too churchy for some AA meetings, but then again, we were meeting in a church.

Mindy and I found that AA meeting especially helpful as we thought about what we would be doing on our trip. A big part of the journey would involve drinking in bars and spending time with people there. Alcohol abuse brings about all kinds of damage in the world. We were worried that writing about our bar experiences might seem to be an endorsement of the abuse of alcohol. To put it in church language, we were afraid we'd "cause someone to stumble."

This evening spent with people who knew better than anyone the damage that alcohol can do showed us that they still share stories about alcohol and drugs. Funny stories. Horrible stories. Dark stories. Telling those stories made people laugh, but also cry -- and sometimes just nod knowingly. It helped people get on with life. We came out of the meeting confident that telling our bar stories wasn't likely to hurt anyone. It might even help.

***

On Sunday night we returned to the Rescue Mission. Kathleen had invited us to join her for the 7:30 "family" service attended primarily by people who were a part of the rehabilitation program. As we entered the chapel, we noticed two men with handheld scanners checking all the residents' name tags..

The blue chairs had hymnals in pockets on their backs, and there was a carved wooden podium and a "Jesus loves you" banner in the front. Mindy sat down near the back of the left side of the room while I talked to a few people. The people around her were agitated. Nobody responded to her friendly smiles, and she began to suspect she'd somehow broken a rule.

Eventually, an embarrassed man told her she was sitting in the men's section. Though married couples and families can sit in a designated area, men and women in the program are supposed to sit in different sections. We were okay with that -- I enjoyed sitting with the guys, and Mindy was happy to sit with Kathleen and the other women.

As the service began, everyone was encouraged to stand, though a few of the guys in the back row remained seated. Two guys with guitars, one bearded, both in their 20s or 30s, led the worship, and we later learned that they were graduates of the rehab program who returned most Sunday nights. A smiling, compact 90-year-old man named Bob, who had served at the rescue mission for more than 30 years, led prayer. He prayed for a blessing on President Obama, the director of the mission, and the pastor of the mission, Jeff.

When Pastor Jeff, a big, bearded man, came forward after the prayer, he asked the congregation to start off the year strong, and then called out "God is good."

The congregation responded, "All the time!"

Jeff intoned, "All the time?" and the congregation responded, "God is good!"

Jeff read a passage from Mark 8 about Jesus healing the blind man. In the story, the blind man is not immediately healed completely. At first, he sees "men looking like trees." Jeff said that many of us have a fuzzy picture of Jesus. We need to go to God's Word to see Jesus clearly. He urged people to commit to read God's Word and to pray throughout the New Year. Appropriately, the service concluded with the chorus, "Open the Eyes of my Heart."

One state was done. So far, so good. Forty-nine states (and fifty-one weeks) to go.

2
THE BARBERSHOP

After Nevada, we spent a week in Arizona, then went on to New Mexico. There was a moment on the drive from Arizona to New Mexico when we were surprised by enormous beauty. We found ourselves in a canyon (not the Grand one, but a pretty great one) and looked at the multicolored walls that begged for climbing. Mindy and I turned to each other and said, "How are we allowed to do this?" We were amazed that we would be spending months to come soaking in the beauty and grandeur of this country.

The drive from New Mexico to Texas wasn't like that. We made a stop in Roswell, where we planned to see space alien wonders, eat something, and spend the night. We enjoyed the tourist things -- not just the statues of space aliens playing poker, but also statues that honored Western heroes John Chisum and Pat Garrett. By 4:00 pm, a chilly wind was blowing over the snow drifts, we were done finding the truth that was out there, and we were ready for dinner. Domino's was near the top of the Yelp rankings for Roswell, so we decided to keep driving to Texas instead.

And driving. And driving. The weather was overcast and dreary, and so was the scenery. We saw the antelope roaming, but no place to stop to eat or sleep. We were tired, hungry, and more than a little cranky. Finally, way after sunset, we came to a town and saw a Pizza Hut/Wing Street next to a Best Western. The combination looked almost as pretty as those canyons in Arizona.

We walked into the motel, and the desk clerk welcomed us, "Howdy, y'all!" We didn't even care that this basic motel cost way more than we'd budgeted.

***

The next morning, we headed to San Antonio (where we stayed in another Best Western -- this one with Texas-shaped waffles). We wanted to walk the Riverwalk, and we did, but we were delighted to discover all the old and distinctive churches in the downtown area. The receptionist at First Presbyterian Church directed us to the beautiful sanctuary where the organist was helping a student practice for the next day's recital.

We marveled at the statues in St. Mary's Catholic Church (the second oldest church in the city). We visited San Fernando Cathedral, where, according to legend, the remains of the Alamo's defenders are interred.

It was the Alamo we came to see. It was strange to find the iconic walls of the fortress in the heart of a modern city. There's no charge to visit the grounds since private groups have raised funds to keep the property open to the public. There's a place on the grounds called the "Alamo Shrine," a chapel filled with artifacts and placards to explain them. Before entering, we saw a sign reading, "No photography in the Shrine."

As we looked at the displays and read fascinating information that would inevitably slip our minds, Mindy pulled out her phone to document the information. You know, with pictures. As Mindy snapped her first memory (no flash, no damage would be done as far as we could tell), a woman with big blonde hair -- I'd guess she was one of the Daughters of the Republic of Texas -- hurried up, and she reproached Mindy with vigor, "No photography! See, here's the sign telling you! This is sacred ground! You wouldn't take pictures inside a church, would you?"

We had, of course, just spent the morning taking pictures in churches. We were planning to spend a whole year taking pictures in churches, often during worship services, but we still haven't gotten over feeling awkward about doing it. Snapping photos in bars usually makes us feel tacky as well. These are places people expect a modicum of privacy, and yet we strangers play paparazzi. Still, we didn't feel too bad about taking pictures to help us remember the Alamo. I doubt Davy Crockett would be too shook up about it.

The next day we drove to Dripping Springs, the Austin suburb where we were going to stay with Julie and Dan, high school friends of mine. Staying with them quickly felt like home.

I should note that Dan and Julie are Catholic, like about one in five Americans. I mention this (awkwardly) because we on the journey we met people who had marked hostility toward the Roman Catholic Church.

In bars, people who were raised in the Catholic Church seemed to talk about it like they'd escaped the Gulag. They called the Church "homophobic" and "anti-woman" and "proponents of hegemony" (okay, I'm not sure that the last one was an exact quote). The other place we heard bad things about Catholics was in churches, particularly in fundamentalist and some evangelical churches. Some seem to think finding "true believers" among Roman Catholics would make a great headline if the *Weekly World News* was still around.

When we started the trip, we said we'd go to any church where they love Jesus. That's pretty much how we decided to define a "good church." We didn't want to go bad churches, and we didn't want to go to any church just for the spectacle. We hoped that by looking for churches and ministries that aim to show love for Jesus and love for people, we'd find those "good" places.

Julie told us about one such ministry, Mobile Loaves & Fishes' Community First! Village, in Austin.

***

We turned into the entrance next to the teepees on Hog Eye Road and parked near assorted older trailers. We wondered if they belonged to workers or if they were used as residences. One of them had an office sign on it, so we knocked. The trailer had three offices in it, and the people working in one section pointed us to Matt, a 30-ish, bearded guy in the back office. Even though, as assistant manager for the property, he had other work to do, he seemed happy for an excuse to go outside and show us around.

Matt told us that Mobile Loaves & Fishes started back in 1998 with five men from a Catholic Church in Austin who filled a minivan with food to feed the homeless. They wanted to do more, and Mobile Loaves & Fishes now has a fleet of modified catering trucks that offer food, clothing, hygiene items, and other life-sustaining material to homeless people in Austin and other nearby communities. But they still wanted to do more, so they decided to create a community where homeless people could find a home.

Tiny houses seem to be a cultural obsession in the United States, though many are watching HGTV's Tiny House programs in rooms as big as a tiny house. But tiny houses provide practical shelter at the Loaves and Fishes. Some of the tiny houses have been donated and built by churches or church groups, and some by construction companies. Matt showed us the community gardens, the farm animals -- and the blacksmith shop, which I especially wanted to see. Residents can learn blacksmithing skills, and Matt told us, "One of our residents makes art projects and sells them. I believe he made more money last year than I did."

This is not a community for everyone. Except for a few missional families, who live in the trailers rather than the tiny houses, residents may not have children living with them. Residents agree to abide by a code of conduct which includes paying rent. Almost everyone who lives in the community, except the missional families, has government assistance which covers the modest rent and other necessary expenses. The challenge for many homeless people, we learned, is to obtain and keep the paperwork that entitles them to receive that assistance.

They also have several tiny chapels, and a larger worship area was under construction. Residents aren't required to go to church, but it's there for them. Residents aren't required to go to the movies, either, but a local chain, Alamo Drafthouse, has built an outdoor theater on the grounds. The Drafthouse donates screenings of current films, and those screenings are open to the broader neighborhood as a goodwill gesture from Community First! Village.

On the organization's website, Alan Graham, the president of Mobile Loaves and Fishes, wrote, "Everything we do is about relationships. The biggest lesson we have learned over the years is that we are not a food ministry. We merely use food as a conduit to connect human to human and heart to heart."

I think my favorite moment was when we passed a house that didn't yet have its siding in place. The pine walls were covered with handwritten Bible verses conveying the hopes and prayers of the builders for the future residents of the home. Matt told us that whenever a resident moves in, there's a blessing ceremony, welcoming the new resident to the community.

***

As we prepared for the trip, people told us Texas is a different kind of state. They said, "The people you see at the bar Saturday night you'll see the next morning at church." That wasn't exactly the way it worked for us, but we did go to the bar with Dan and Julie on Thursday night and to church Sunday morning.

The Barbershop got its name because that's what the building was for twenty-five years. Before that, it was a garage and gas station, but now it's a popular brewpub. When we arrived Thursday evening, the parking places on the street nearby were nearly filled. (We overheard a local say, "Some of the hardest parking ever.")

A group of guys sitting at an outside table seemed to have started on their beer much earlier and were enjoying themselves. When a car whizzed by, they let their displeasure be known,
"Speed limit's 25 miles per hour, dude!"

"It should be ten."

"They should patrol here on Mercer. They don't need it anywhere else!"

Dan and Julie had said they'd meet us later, so we walked in and soaked in the kitsch: deer heads, barber poles, and bright neon beer signs. We saw a plaque from the Dripping Springs Chamber of Commerce a few years before, honoring the bar as Business of the Year. I enjoyed watching people struggle with the front door, which had a knob requiring just the right amount of pressure before opening. The chalkboard that tallies the number of people who come in looking for a haircut was a favorite running gag for the initiated (the count that night was 184).

Many bars claim to welcome all, but here that "all" was a little more inclusive. We saw a couple of children in the bar (which apparently is okay as far as the local law was concerned -- and the kids were with adults), and dogs were welcome too. Julie and Dan joined us, and we spent some time chatting and enjoying our beers. (Well, Mindy and I had cider. We don't like beer. We were beginning to see a flaw in our bar-visiting plans.)

I noticed that the bartender was having a good time with the customers, joking and laughing. She was doing a great job solo taking care of a long line of customers while also cleaning up the glasses and cans. Her long dark hair flowed onto her dark work shirt, and she wore a long black skirt. When Alisha had a moment free, I introduced myself. She seemed amused by our quest to go to a church and bar in every state, and she answered my questions between drink orders.

She said, "A good bar should make you feel at home. I know the name of most everyone who comes in here, and I know what they drink, so I'll have it waiting for them. Oh, and beer. We have a lot of choices of good beers."

I also asked what would make for a good church. She asked for clarification so I said, "What would a church have to do to make you want to go there?" She answered, "What would make me want to go to church? That's a hard one. Maybe if it was open-minded and let you share your thoughts and feelings without being judged. I lived in Utah with the Mormons and New Mexico with the Catholics, and I've been with the Baptists. If you'd convert to be like them, they'd be all over that. But I wanted them to just accept me for me." Then Alisha was off to take more orders.

***

Mindy and Julie headed back to the house to work on dinner, while Dan and I stayed to talk some more. Dan is a couple of years older than Julie and Mindy and me but doesn't look it. When I wrote earlier about people who aren't fond of the Catholic Church in this country, I didn't mention one of the big problems people have with Catholicism, something I wanted to talk to Dan about: the pedophile scandals that rocked the Church the last few decades, and which continue to reverberate.

In bars and Protestant churches, many people cited the abuse as the reason they left the Catholic Church. (Of course, abuse like this isn't limited to the Catholic Church. Many Protestant churches have experienced such things. In fact, Healdsburg Community Church, where I served, went through such a painful episode in the years before we came. After that, the church established procedures to protect children from abuse.)

Sexual abuse still happens in churches, mosques, and synagogues. But it also happens in public schools. The greater scandal in the Catholic Church was not even the abuse, but the cover-up of the abuse which cast a shadow not just on individuals but the church as a whole. It was evil. I could understand why people would look at such actions and decide to leave the church. But I learned Dan personally observed some horrible things in the church but stayed. I wanted to talk to him about that decision.

Dan told me he'd grown up in a family deeply committed to the Catholic Church. His drill sergeant father, a man of great faith, made sure they were at Mass every Sunday, but Dan hadn't internalized that faith growing up. When Dan was eighteen, he went to a Catholic charismatic renewal meeting at a church in Santa Rosa. There, he really understood God's Word and felt changed by God's grace. There was an altar call, and he was the first to go forward.

The change in his life was dramatic. He sold all that he had and left California to join the priest who'd led the renewal meetings to minister in Wisconsin. Dan helped lead worship, playing the guitar on a tour of churches. He had a wonderful time. Dan continued to stay with the same priest. One night the priest asked Dan to join him on his bed. The priest didn't make an explicit proposition, but Dan didn't join him on the bed. Instead, he returned to Santa Rosa.

The priests in Dan's local parish thought Dan was destined for priesthood himself, and they encouraged him to pursue the calling. But Dan continued to see things that just weren't right. He lived in a house with another priest who brought a series of young women to his room. Since the door was closed, Dan never actually knew what went on, but he didn't like it.

Dan's parents had always put the clergy on a pedestal, but for Dan, the pedestal had been kicked away. He began to feel that perhaps his faith was a farce. He went through a dark time of questioning.

After Dan married Julie, the option of becoming a priest was gone, but Julie and Dan remained very active in their church. Sadly, episodes of clerical misconduct continued as well. The most severe blow was when Dan learned that someone very close to him had been sexually abused by a priest. Dan changed parishes but continued to raise his family in the Catholic Church and to seek God's truth in Scripture.

Years later, Dan again experienced great spiritual darkness and considered chucking the church along with his faith and his whole life as he knew it. He went on a retreat, where a spiritual mentor suggested meditating on a prayer, the Chaplet of Divine Mercy, focusing on Christ's sacrifice. As Dan prayed, he asked God, "Where are you now?"

Dan said it was then that God's grace fell upon him. He heard the words, "I'm still here." He felt God take the hurt that had built up over the years. He felt God tell him to go home and love his family.

Dan said he's come to realize that in God's eyes clergy are no more sacred than garbage collectors and just as susceptible to sin. Jesus called the religious leaders of His time "whitewashed tombs," but the sins of those men didn't invalidate the teaching of the Law and the Prophets. Dan still accepts the teaching of the church as true, even if many of the teachers are flawed.

Dan and Julie are active at Saint Catherine of Siena in Austin. They are sponsors in RCIA (Rite of Christian Initiation of Adults), a program that teaches doctrine and practice to those hoping to become a part of the church. The morning we attended Mass with them, Julie was reading the Scripture. The church conducts six masses every weekend with a different reader for each service. Those readers get together during the week to study the Scripture for the upcoming weekend.

Dan and Julie spoke fondly of their parish priest, Father Pat, and his assistant, Father Ray. Father Ray was home visiting family in India the Sunday we visited, and parish policy doesn't allow a priest to lead more than three masses a weekend, so we heard a homily from Father Charlie. Charlie is in his 80's and was still quite active in prison ministry. Father Charlie has the cadence of a Southern Baptist radio preacher and a love of acronyms (LOVE - Live on Victoriously Eternally, GOD - Good Orderly Direction, JOY - Jesus first, Others next, Yourself last, etc.) Though Julie and Dan admitted they'd heard Father Charlie give the same message before, they expressed admiration for the man's love and faithfulness.

I asked Dan what he would say to those who quit going to church because they can't forgive the actions of the Catholic clergy, particularly the incidents of child abuse. He said he would tell them to repeat the "Our Father" (that's the Lord's prayer for us Protestants), meditating on every word, and concentrate on the passage on forgiveness. "We can't hold a grudge or pass judgment on others. When we do, we put a wall up between ourselves and God."

***

We left Austin, but we weren't done with Texas yet. We made a long, spur of the moment detour to the small town of Archer to see the bookstore owned by one of my favorite writers, Larry McMurtry of Lonesome Dove fame. We arrived to find the bookstore closed. The store is only open Thursday through Saturday, and we'd arrived on Monday. A manager working inside saw us peering in the window and taking pictures from across the street, and she graciously let us in to browse for a few minutes. We purchased a "Booked Up" bumper sticker for our van and had lunch at the Dairy Queen immortalized in a book of McMurtry's essays.

We were also able to visit one of my old youth group students, Chase, who was a prison guard. He introduced us to his boss, Bud, who doesn't just work as a correctional officer but also pastors a church. Bud and Chase told us that many guards have schedules that make it difficult to attend typical Sunday morning worship, so Bud's church planned early morning breakfast meetings for guards immediately after or just before shifts (at 4:30 or 5:00 am). We were sorry to miss one of those worship services, but we needed to get to McKinney, on the outskirts of Dallas, to meet an old friend from a comic book store.

When we lived in the Santa Cruz area, we frequented a comic book store called Atlantis Fantasyworld, which was unique for a couple of reasons. For one thing, it's the store featured in the movie *The Lost Boys*. It's also longer lived than most comic book stores -- when we moved to the area, it was over twenty years old, and it's still around.

On our first visit to Atlantis, our daughter Paige was in second grade and began to wander toward the "Adult" section (not porn comics, but comics with what they call "mature content," like violence and nakedness). Being more observant than we were, a young woman with a bright red pixie haircut hurried from behind the counter saying, "You'll really like what's over here," and redirecting her toward the kid-friendly material. (Sadly for us, it might have been Pokemon.)

That's how we met Maryanne, and she won us over that day. She married and eventually moved to Texas, but we kept in touch via Facebook. Though her husband Bruce (whom we still haven't met) was out of town, we were glad to get to stay with Maryanne and meet her children. At Liberty Burger (obviously a Texas kind of place), Maryanne told us that Bruce had read about Alisha, the bartender at The Barbershop, and how Mormons and Baptists had ignored her when she didn't join their church. He'd used the story in a Sunday School class he was teaching. He and Maryanne are members of the Church of Jesus Christ of Latter-day Saints, and Alisha's story illustrated a point Bruce wanted to make about acceptance.

Mindy and I found this very encouraging. Perhaps writing and posting about churches, bars, and movies wasn't going out into a black void, but maybe people were reading it -- and finding our experiences in bars and churches helpful.

As we left Maryanne's house, though, we wondered what the coming weeks in the deep South might have in store for us. We'd already disagreed where we should go. Though we had friends and family in some of the upcoming states, Mindy was concerned about the debauchery in a state not too far away.

3
THE FRENCH QUARTER

Mindy and I had a difference of opinion about where we should go in Louisiana. Mindy was reluctant about a place where the exchange of a bead necklace for a flash of breasts seemed to be a common transaction, and where Hurricanes (a rum drink that seemed to be invented to get tourists sloshed quickly) were celebrated.

I thought we should hit as many iconic pieces of Americana as we could along the way, and New Orleans certainly qualified. The city has a unique place in popular culture and U.S. history, and I figured it was a must for the trip. Plus, the music and the food were famous.

More than anything else, the undercurrent of the occult (voodoo, fortune tellers and such) made Mindy think of it as a sad, dark place, and she wasn't sure she wanted to go there.

Since we had such different views on the subject, we'd avoided deciding while we were planning the trip. We didn't know anyone in the state, and we mostly decided our destinations with a very simple question: Do we know anyone in this state who'll give us a place to sleep?

Just three weeks into the trip, our thinking about New Orleans changed. At Eldorado Community Church in New Mexico, Jake (a guy in the worship band who did a great Jurassic Park riff on guitar) asked me, "Do you have any place to go in Louisiana?"

I said, "No."

He said we had to go to Vieux Carre Baptist Church in New Orleans' French Quarter. He told us he'd gone there on a missions trip, and he raved about the place. "And they have rooms for the people who come to work, so you could probably sleep at the church." He gave us Pastor Tom Bilderback's email address, and we sent off a query.

Tom responded quickly, telling us that no other groups were scheduled when we'd be there, so we were welcome to stay in bunk beds at the church. He told us that the church asked guests to pay $15.00 a night (I wasn't clear on whether that was $15.00 for one of us or both of us, but either way it was a bargain). So we were going to New Orleans, and I won that one.

Not that marriage is a competition. At all. Wouldn't be healthy.

***

As we headed through Louisiana, we started hearing thunderstorm warnings. After we turned eastward toward Baton Rouge, frequent thunderclaps and the steady, rapid swish of the windshield wipers almost kept us from hearing radio warnings about tornadoes in parishes (they're parishes in Louisiana, not counties, we learned) that were probably nearby.

We considered finding a place to pull over, but with the heavy rain, we were concerned that the roadside would flood. Eventually, we arrived at our motel a few blocks from the New Orleans airport and turned on the TV. We learned that earlier in the afternoon, a tornado -- one of a record number in southeastern Louisiana and southern Mississippi that day -- had touched down half a mile away.

Wednesday morning the weather cleared up, and we drove into the city. We needed to watch our movie in a theater, and we'd discovered a special 75th-anniversary screening of *The Maltese Falcon* playing at the Theaters at Canal Place, a swanky shopping destination with Tiffany's and Saks 5th Avenue among its attractions. The theater -- and the ticket price -- was upscale as well, which worried us.

Once in the intimate screening room, we received a menu with things like a hummus trio and crawfish and avocado dip. The most ordinary popcorn was topped with white truffle oil. We stretched out in our reclining seats and tried to enjoy the movie instead of fretting about money.

After the movie, we had plenty of time to find Vieux Carre Baptist Church before Wednesday night Bible study. We walked to Jackson Square and looked into St. Louis Cathedral. Like almost every cathedral we saw during the year, the stained glass, soaring ceiling, and hush took our breath away.

Going out again and finding ourselves on Bourbon Street was something of a shock. It was Wednesday afternoon a few weeks after Mardi Gras, and the bars were bustling and noisy. A block away, Dauphine Street was quieter, with fewer bars. One was next door to the church.

Vieux Carre Baptist was a little more difficult to spot than, say, St. Louis Cathedral. A simple metal sign shaped like an open Bible hung over the door. When we got there, the doors were open and around a dozen people, mostly men, were sitting around a table in the main room. We recognized Pastor Tom, a bearded man we guessed to be in his 40s. Three other out-of-town visitors about our age, pastors from Texas, were visiting the church as research for an upcoming missions trip.

Jason, a brown-haired man with bandages on his hands, introduced himself, mentioning that he was homeless and an alcoholic. Tom came over and asked him, "Where's your buddy? Where's Joey?"

Jason answered, "Either in jail or in the hospital."

Tom nodded and said, "We'll hope he's in jail, then." (That did turn out to be Joey's location, which was a relief.)

Before heading back to the motel for the night, we learned that we might be able to use one of the three parking spots in front of the church the next day. Parking can be tricky in many big cities, but in New Orleans, particularly the French Quarter, it can be a real nightmare. Not only is parking scarce, but many spaces are also unmarked and getting towed is expensive. But on Thursdays from 11:00 am to 1:00 pm, the four spaces on Dauphin Street in front of Vieux Carre Baptist are empty for street cleaning -- after that, it's first come, first served, and cars can stay there until the street's cleaned again.

We checked out of our motel room on Thursday around noon and were delighted when we snagged one of the parking spots. We decided we wouldn't move the van until we left on Sunday; if we wanted to go somewhere, we'd walk. (Others connected with the church park blocks away and have to move their vehicles frequently. Since we carried most of our earthly belongings in the minivan, this was not an attractive option.)

Sorting shoes was our assignment for the afternoon. The church had a collection of donated shoes, and we needed to separate the men's and women's shoes, sort them by size, and put them away in the clothes closet. Mainly, though, we needed to throw shoes away. The women's shoes were in pretty good shape, because women are more likely, as a rule, to donate shoes while they still have life in them. Many of the men's donated shoes were thrashed -- some even had holes in the soles. Some women's shoes weren't worth keeping on the shelves, but more because four-inch heels might not be ideal footwear for life on the streets.

Tom told us that the church began as a home Bible study back in 1954, moving from house to house. The current building was purchased in 1964 (there were conflicting reports -- it had been either a restaurant or a bakery). Several pastors have served there through the years, one of whom was not even Baptist; at times, the church didn't have a pastor.

Decades ago, one pastor was so irritated by loud jukebox music from the bar next door that he stopped in the middle of his Sunday morning sermon, went next door and demanded they turn down the music. The music, not surprisingly for the French Quarter, was turned up. When the pastor went back with a knife and cut the jukebox cord, the bar called the cops. The pastor had to repair the cord to avoid being arrested.

Since then, The Vieux's relationship with its neighbors has become much more cordial. During Mardi Gras parades, members of the Vieux stood on their gallery and threw Moon Pies to people on the floats. (A "gallery" is like a balcony, but there's a distinction that only seems to be clear to residents of NOLA.) Tom said many in the community expected judgment from the Church, but they appreciated getting some "sugar" instead.

The connection of the church to the Southern Baptist Conference is somewhat loose, but the church stays true to the conference's doctrinal positions. Some of those tenets differ significantly from the values of the community, but the church emphasizes the love of Jesus.

Tom came to New Orleans in 2007 after years of working as a master auto mechanic. He got a job as a bartender on Bourbon Street and joined the congregation at Vieux Carre Baptist, but he wasn't (yet) the pastor. Though he doesn't have a seminary background (in fact, he doesn't have a college background), his heart and gifts are those of a pastor,. He was called to serve the church in 2011.

***

Tom's also one of the rare pastors we felt we could trust for a bar recommendation. We didn't want to go to Bourbon Street since we were looking for a local bar rather than a tourist mecca. Tom had worked at the Tropical Island, home of the "Hand Grenade," and he didn't recommend it. (Hand Grenades are a mix of gin, rum, vodka, grain alcohol and melon liqueur served in tacky plastic cups shaped like green grenades.) Instead, he sent us to Buffa's on the corner of Esplanade and Burgundy, at the northern corner of the Quarter.

We had our choice of two rooms at Buffa's: the front room had the bar, but the live entertainment was in the back room. The rooms are connected by a corridor, and we knew this was the place for us when we saw the plethora of *Doctor Who*, *Firefly*, and Monty Python posters decorating the hallway. Alexandra Scott was in the back room singing "The Rubber Ducky Song" (she sounded very different than *Sesame Street*'s Ernie), followed by a Tom Waits tune, but we decided to sit at the bar in the front room instead.

We were soon chatting with Holly, the bartender, who had bright red hair, a big smile, and that night, a Tom Waits shirt (I don't know if she'd checked in with Alexandra before dressing). We told her we wanted to spend the evening with New Orleans locals rather than tourists, and Holly assured us she qualified. She'd moved from Las Vegas just six weeks before Katrina. A few days after the storm she was bussed off to another location but returned as soon as she could.

She told us that according to local lore, anyone who weathered Katrina is grandfathered in as a New Orleans native. She's obviously proud of her status and proud of the city. She loves the food and the music and the drinks. She said she never knew what life was about until she came.

We asked Holly the two questions we always ask in bars, "What makes for a good bar?" and "What makes for a good church?" She said, "Drinks are the least important element of a good bar." She looks for a place that's fun, with music and a good vibe. She loves Buffa's but has other favorites in the Quarter such as Cosimo's and the Golden Lantern (it should be noted neither is on Bourbon Street). The Golden Lantern is a gay-friendly bar, and she enjoys the burlesque drag shows.

She isn't a church-goer, but the Golden Lantern had Gospel Drag Shows on Sundays. She said they're fun and "that's where I get my Jesus on."

*****

I had to be up early the next morning to go to Louis Armstrong Park in the Treme (just across Rampart Street from the French Quarter) with Tom. It's a beautiful park, with statues not only of Satchmo but other jazz greats along with beautiful foliage, fountains, and ponds. The park is locked up at night, but Tom and I were there when the gates opened at 7:00 am. The little crowd at the entrance was waiting for the tickets Tom had in his pockets, tickets that entitled the holder to a hot shower, lunch, and (depending on availability) clothes from the closet.

It was a chilly morning in February, and I noticed a man wearing shorts and a thin, worn dress shirt and Oxfords past their prime. He watched us from a distance, hesitant to approach. I went over, said hi, and asked if he was interested in a shower (I could see a shave wouldn't hurt either). He told me he'd just gotten out of jail the night before and could really use a jacket. I called to Tom who assured him a jacket was certainly in the realm of possibilities, and he gave the man a ticket. By 8:00 am, most of Tom's 60 or so shower tickets were gone.

Before the church doors opened for showers at 10:30, Tom assigned our jobs. He'd be at the front door, "Doing the politicking," he called it. Adam (a former intern and current church member) was to control the flow at the door to the showers. Along with several other volunteers, I'd be dishing out the jambalaya cooked by Mississippi firefighters who'd provided the day's lunch. Mindy worked in the clothes closet with Mama Rose. Short and sturdy, with her little white dog Gracie at her feet, Rose let Mindy know not to be too trusting of guests who needed supplies. "They take what you give them; don't let them pick and choose. If they ask for shoes, you look at the shoes they're wearing to be sure they really need new ones."

Mama Rose lived on the streets for years, but her life turned around when she became a Christian a few years ago. I talked to one woman who'd known her back in the day. "A man was harassing me, and Mama Rose told him to stop. He didn't. So she decked him." Mama Rose is a vital part of the ministry of the Vieux, and Tom's wife Sonja said that Rose had been more of a mother to her, in some ways, than her own mother.

One woman with a shower ticket was allowed inside before 10:30. Her name was Baby Doll, and Sonja explained that she took a long time in the women's shower, so for everyone's convenience, she was allowed in early. Baby Doll brought her bike with its decorated wagon into the church's entry hall for security, where it remained for a day or so. Sonja told us that Baby Doll used to have a vile temper, but she said that God had worked in her heart. Over time, she's become a sweetheart.

During the 10:30 shower session, I served lunch next to Chris, a volunteer who attended a church in Metairie. She asked about our trip and asked if we had any place to stay in Mississippi, our next state. When I said no, she pulled out her phone and made a call. Before the next shower session, a youth pastor in Long Beach, Mississippi, had arranged a place to stay, and we knew what church we'd be visiting. Chris also invited us to her house for authentic New Orleans food, with a bonus lesson in area history and geography from her husband. We were grateful for all of it.

Later, my assignment was to eat lunch and chat with folks around the table. I listened to stories about what brought them to the city. Part of the appeal of the area is the relatively mild climate (apart from the occasional tornado, hurricane, or flood). Sadly, a bigger draw for many was the ready availability of drugs and alcohol. When money or other people's patience wore out, the streets of New Orleans had a new resident.

After the second shower session, when all the guests had left, I headed to my bunk to read when I noticed Mindy cleaning the shower stalls in the women's room. "I have to use it," she said. "I figured I'd better clean it." Which meant, of course, I'd have to do the same.

The men's room was just a few steps down the narrow hallway, and the overpowering stench hit me before I got to the door. It was the smell of 60 - 70 men showering for the first time in a long time. The floor was littered with socks, underwear, paper plates, styrofoam cups, and a cookie. (I heard much stranger and more disgusting things were found in other weeks.) The worst area was around the sinks where the stubble from men who hadn't shaved for a while was bad, but the blood mixed in was worse.

I put on gloves and went to work with my friend Mr. Bleach. As I was scrubbing, Tom walked in, and I don't know if his look of shock was real or feigned. He said, "What are you doing here? Usually, pastors find something better to do after lunch." My respect for Tom and other folks who clean those restrooms week in and week out is great.

Mindy started running the washing machine. Most people who get clothes leave behind what they were wearing. Everything (except the underwear) got washed in really hot water and bleach, then put back into the closet. After all the clothes and towels were washed, she ran a load with just bleach.

***

Shower Friday is one of the reasons the smell of bleach will always bring New Orleans to mind. A little before 7:00 am Saturday morning, I found another when we crossed Bourbon Street. The street was covered with garbage -- hurricane glasses, those hand grenades, and cups from Jesters shaped like jesters (Mindy and I often scavenged plastic souvenir cups after Oakland A's games. We weren't tempted to scavenge here at all) mixed with all the gooey detritus of a long night of bar hopping. Trucks scooped the garbage from the streets and sprayed bleach behind them to deal with the, um, biological waste. I can't say I love the smell of bleach in the morning (I mean, it's no napalm), but we were glad to see those bleach trucks.

We returned to the street late that afternoon, enjoying the buskers (street entertainers). Along with the musicians, magicians, and jugglers, we saw people with typewriters offering original poems, composed and typed on the spot. We thought we might be able to do that when our money ran out.

That evening, we walked by a woman painted green, the paint distracting me momentarily from the fact she was topless. Walking by the "Barely Legal" sign of the Hustler Club made me sad, and I guess it was obvious. A barker called out, "Cheer up! You're on Bourbon Street!"

***

On Sunday morning, we decided to get beignets before church, but we'd forgotten about the Rock and Roll Marathon. We waited until there was a gap between the runners on Decatur Street and crossed over to Cafe du Monde. There's probably a rule that everybody who goes to New Orleans has to get beignets and coffee from Cafe du Monde. That's why they're open 24 hours a day, and there's always a line.

We were in line behind two women wearing number bibs who seemed to have taken a break in their run. When they got to the front of the line, they were disappointed to realize that Cafe du Monde is cash only -- no credit cards. They had to go back to the race hungry.

We got back to the Vieux in plenty of time for the Sunday service. The church doors open at 8:00 am for donuts and coffee, though the service doesn't start until 10:30. (The services start a half hour earlier during the NFL season for Saints fans. Service time may also vary due to festivals. It doesn't take much for the church to be closed off to traffic. Streets in the French Quarter are narrow.) Some locals came in just for the snacks, but folks from the congregation were around to talk to anybody who came in the door.

In fact, so many good conversations were going on that the service started around ten minutes late. Guest musicians led worship. Tom preached an excellent sermon on "The Trouble with Being Naked" from Genesis 3. Tom may not have college or seminary training, but he is well read, and his teaching was both intellectually and personally challenging. (The trouble with being naked, by the way, is that as a result of sin, we want to hide who we are from God and other people.)

After church, we headed out to the minivan to drive on to Mississippi, leaving our parking space for someone else. Lauren, an intern who lived at the church, came out with us.

Lauren had already given us one of our favorite quotes of the entire year. I'd asked her what she liked about the church. "Honesty," she answered. "Every other church I've been in, people try to act like they have it all together." The guys on the street don't hide their problems, like people in the church do. They're alcoholics and addicts. They can't pretend they have it all together.

 And now Lauren gave us another gift -- a "NOLA (New Orleans, Louisiana) 'til I die" bumper sticker. At that point in the year, there was still plenty of room on the back of the van for more stickers, and she put hers in a prominent spot on the right-hand side. By December, the back of the minivan would be well covered.

People ask us, "What was your favorite church?" It isn't prudent to answer that question because we met so many people in wonderful ministries, and it's not fair to rank them. Anyway, don't tell the other churches, but Vieux Carre Baptist Church was our favorite on the trip.

But according to everybody we'd talked to, New Orleans wasn't really the deep south. We'd need to keep going to learn more, so we headed east.

4
16TH STREET BAPTIST CHURCH

The next week, at the Baptist church in Long Beach, Mississippi, we mentioned that we hoped to visit 16th Street Baptist Church in Birmingham, and something odd came up. I think three different people said, "I hope you're welcomed there." They expressed concern that white people would be shunned in a black church.

I can't imagine people in California asking if we'd be welcomed in a black church. It's not that I think there's a racism free zone by the Pacific, it just doesn't seem like something that would occur to most people (and the norms of politically correct speech would certainly deter people from saying anything). In the South, issues of race -- particularly betweens blacks and whites -- percolated closer to the surface of things. I'm pretty sure history has something to do with it.

We arrived in Alabama a year after the 50th anniversary of Martin Luther King Junior's historic marches from Selma to Montgomery to support the right of African Americans to vote. We drove the route, but in reverse, starting in Montgomery at the church where Dr. King served as a pastor, now known as the Dexter Avenue King Memorial Baptist Church. It's a charming red brick building within sight of the state capitol building steps. There is something satisfying about knowing that strategies for oppression and strategies for freedom were being plotted within a distance of a few hundred yards of each other.

At the Edmund Pettus Bridge in Selma, where police had attacked marchers with billy clubs and tear gas (on a day which came to be known as Bloody Sunday), we found a souvenir shop and some memorials. We bought a few postcards from the elderly black woman who ran the shop, and she told us that the place had swarmed with people for the 50th anniversary of the event the year before. It was quiet now; the shelves and counters of the makeshift store held a lot of memorabilia commemorating Dr. King and the Selma march as well as quite a few items honoring President Obama.

We walked around the memorial and under the bridge, then drove to Brown Chapel A.M.E. Church where the march had begun. Signs mark the building as historical, and rightly so, but the aging one-story apartments across the street and to one side of the church, which were probably built around the time of the march, just looked old. We wondered what role race played in the economics of the neighborhood.

Back in New Orleans, Mindy and I had taken a walk across Rampart Street into the Treme neighborhood. We'd passed people chatting on their front stoops in the February sunshine. They'd waved and said hello, and we'd waved back. When we passed Saint Augustine Catholic Church, we walked around the building hoping to be able to look inside, but instead, we found the Tomb of the Unknown Slave. It's a cross constructed of chains and shackles that honors the uncounted and unnamed men and women who perished as slaves. We'd been surprised and moved by the unexpected memorial.

Here, though, we felt sad and didn't want to stare at the homes or people; even taking pictures of the church felt tacky. We took a few quick photos of the church and hurried back to the minivan. Still, the community seemed to take pride in the church itself, in spite of the litter blowing around in the street.

***

The 16th Street Baptist Church in Birmingham was another church with an important place in American civil rights history. In 1950's and '60's Birmingham, there were numerous demonstrations to oppose segregation and Jim Crow laws. The Reverend Fred Shuttlesworth of Birmingham co-founded the Southern Christian Leadership Conference, and Dr. King was invited to the city (where he was famously jailed). Perhaps the most iconic incident of the movement in Birmingham was the bombing of

16th Street Baptist Church resulting in the deaths of four young women. The horror of that event became national news and helped lead to the Civil Rights Act of 1964. We were looking forward to visiting it, but we were concerned that it might be more of a monument than a living body.

A quick look at the church's website convinced us with these words: "When all is said and done, all that we aspire to BE and all we attempt to DO is intended to glorify Jesus through the power and presence of the Holy Spirit to the glory of God the Father. Jesus really is our MAIN ATTRACTION. He is the reason we are!"

We decided to visit the Wednesday evening Bible Study, but we arrived early and walked around Kelly Ingram Park across from the church. The park is dedicated as a place of revolution and reconciliation because of its place in the Civil Rights movement of the 1960s. Among statues commemorating terrible, brutal events where police attacked demonstrating children with fire hoses and dogs, another statue caught our attention. It's called "The Four Spirits," and it's a memorial to the four girls killed at the church. Written at the base of the statue were the words, "A love that forgives."

There weren't many people in the park, but we noticed a photographer by a sculpture representing the jail cell where the protesters (as young as six years old) were imprisoned. A well-dressed woman who looked a few years older than us was posing inside, and we were curious. After they finished, we asked what the pictures were for, and the woman told us she'd been arrested when she was fifteen and held in the jail because of her support of the movement during the protests the park honored.

It was getting dark, so we headed back to church for Bible Study, even though we were early. The main doors were locked, as were the downstairs doors where tourists could enter the museum (during the hours noted on the door...which were long past by this time). Eventually, we followed a couple carrying bags of food through a side door.

This couple welcomed us when we explained why we were there, and led us into a downstairs room with display cases along the sides and photographs of former pastors covering one wall. They dropped off the groceries in a kitchen and led us to a meeting room where a dozen or more people sat on folding chairs around a table.

A striking woman wearing a business suit was reading on a pew set along the back wall. She asked about us and answered some of our questions about the church. We should have realized -- certainly when she told us her name, but also because of the gracious way she made us feel welcome -- that she was the pastor's wife, Candie Price. In fact, she literally wrote the book on being a pastor's wife: *First Lady: The Real Truth*. She told us that the people sitting around the table were Sunday School teachers. Every Wednesday, the teachers for the children, youth, and adults meet before Bible Study to discuss the Scripture that will be studied in class on Sunday.

Kenneth Hicks, an associate minister at the church, led the Sunday school teachers' class. When a woman commented on the divinity of Christ, he said, "That's good theology!" as he did when a man noted we are saved by grace through faith and not through works. The teachers were studying Mark 10, focusing on the story of the rich, young ruler, discussing the meaning of the story, how to present the message, and how to apply it to adults and teens and children. We were really interested in this method of keeping the whole church focused on the same message.

When the meeting was over, it was time for the Bible Study, led by the Reverend Arthur Price, Jr. (Candie's husband). He was teaching on the first chapters of Ezekiel, and if you know that book of the Bible, you know it's a challenge. For example, in Ezekiel 1: 4 - 7: "I looked, and I saw a windstorm coming out of the north -- an immense cloud with flashing lightning and surrounded by brilliant light. The center of the fire looked like glowing metal and in the fire was what looked like four living creatures. In appearance their form was human but each of them had four faces and four wings." NIV) Rev. Price was willing to challenge his people with the opaque imagery and the grim foretelling of judgement, and he brought clarity and practical application to these daunting passages.

***

After the meeting, we asked Rev. Hicks if there was any kind of volunteer work we could do at the church over the next couple of days. He said there was nothing we could do at their church but suggested we contact the Jimmie Hale Mission (we'd already noticed the billboards as we drove around town).

When we called, the folks at the mission said we could help serve lunch and dinner. Chaplain Conrad gave us a quick tour and told us about the rehabilitation program, which a success rate of about 12% "because alcohol and drugs are deadly masters. You don't see old drug addicts. There is pure heroin on the streets of Birmingham, and one hot shot can kill a man."

Jimmie Hale Mission began in a storefront work in 1944, the dream of Jimmie Hale, an alcoholic who came to trust in Christ. He wanted to serve the homeless and the poor, but died just a few months later at the age of 39. His wife Jessie and a man named Leo Shepura continued his work, and today the mission serves thousands of men, women, and children at several different facilities. We visited the Shepura Men's Center where over 300 meals are served daily to overnight guests and the men who are part of the rehabilitation program.

We got to the kitchen, and I'll admit serving the mashed potatoes was tricky. I was having a hard time getting the proper amount of spuds on the plates because they were sticking to the scoop, but one of the veterans in the line told me to give the scoop a good whack on the plate -- it probably wouldn't break. This turned out to be sound advice.

Chaplain Conrad had told us the Center's best work was discipling men "in the knowledge and wisdom of Jesus Christ and the Word of God." Conrad had served as a pastor in several churches but said that the last five years of ministry at Jimmy Hale had been "the best gig" of his life.

***

On Friday afternoon, we took the official tour of 16th Street Baptist Church. The charge for the tour was $5 a person, which was at the upper end of what we allowed ourselves for tours and museums. We made exceptions, but not often.

The tour started in the same basement room where we'd met for Bible Study, and our group was mostly college students. After looking (but, as requested, not taking photos) in a narrow room fitted up as a museum of 16th Street's part in the Civil Rights movement, we were taken upstairs to the sanctuary for a video about the church's history. It told the story of the church as a staging area for marches and protests, and the tragedy on September 15, 1963 when the four girls, aged 11 - 14, were murdered with a bomb planted just outside the church's side door (the bomb had gone off just a few feet from where we'd entered the church for Bible Study). Like almost everything at the church, praising God was an integral part of the history.

Since we'd had the preview of the Sunday School lesson about the rich young ruler on Wednesday night, we figured we needed to go to Sunday School. We found ourselves in a building next to the church (it was the parsonage until 1960) where the married couples class met. Jackie, who we'd met on Wednesday night, welcomed us as friends, not strangers.

We talked about how the rich young ruler had gone away sad when Jesus told him to give away his possessions. Professor Brown, a well-dressed man in his 60s, introduced his thoughts by saying, "Confession is good for the soul, but bad for your reputation." He said he'd read that a professional man should have seven suits; he was startled to realize he had closer to seventy. He wondered if maybe this Scripture passage, for him, meant that he should give up some suits.

All of us in the class were between 50 and 65 years old, and except for Mindy and me, African-Americans who had successful careers. As a group, we how all of us were wealthy by worldwide standards. I don't remember whether we discussed local standards of wealth, but we agreed that it was important to welcome people of all economic classes, especially the poor, into the church rather than using wealth to segregate ourselves.

After class was over, we went into the sanctuary, where (as obvious visitors) we were offered a visitor's card. We filled it out and handed it to the usher when he came back for it. Visitors (we were among about 30 others that morning) were welcomed by name and asked to stand.

Also standing was a group of students from East Mecklenburg, a public high school in Charlotte, North Carolina. A group from that school visits the church every year as part of their civil rights history studies.

To be honest, we were hoping for a big gospel choir in flashy robes, blowing the roof off with a big, rousing sound. Instead the choral music that morning came from a children's choir and a youth choir who were joined by the congregation, making the service more of a worship experience than an entertainment experience.

That Sunday, Rev. Price was finishing a six-part series, "Resetting the Ministry," studying the miracles of Jesus in the Gospel of John, with a sermon about the resurrection of Lazarus from John 11. Rev. Price asked the congregation if they'd experienced unwanted delays, frustration, and tragedy in life, and there were loud exclamations of agreement.

He concluded the sermon with a enlightening illustration about taking his wife to McDonald's during their dating days. He said he'd learned that if he ordered straight from the menu, the order always came quickly. But if he made a special order ("Hold the onions, mayo instead of secret sauce"), they would write his name on the ticket, and the order took longer. The delay was there to make things right, which he said is also the reason God sometimes delays an answer to prayer, to get things right.

16th Street Baptist has many of the same challenges faced by other big city churches. Over the years members moved from downtown to the suburbs and stopped coming. For the poor and homeless in the neighborhood, the church's unique position as a tourist destination might be a hindrance to a sense of belonging.

I'm sure a good portion of visitors come to appreciate history rather than worship God, but they end up being there for worship and they hear Jesus glorified. That's a good thing in my book.

There have been -- and continue to be -- great injustices toward people of color in this country. Some churches made some horrible choices -- some in the South defending, even advocating racism. Churches like this one took a stand for Jesus and for His people. These churches made our country a better place.

***

Tensions between blacks and whites, even in the church, aren't gone.

It's strange as a Yankee to visit the South and see monuments to the Confederacy. In Georgia, we went with friends to visit Stone Mountain, which has a monument like Mount Rushmore carved into one side, but with Stonewall Jackson, Robert E. Lee, and Jefferson Davis in the rock. We saw various monuments like this throughout the trip, and I felt torn by the desire to see history preserved while also knowing that people feel real pain seeing ugly values celebrated.

Uglier still were the billboards we'd seen as we drove through the outskirts of Harrison, Arkansas. One read, "It's Not Racist to 'Heart' Your People - WhitePrideRadio.com." Another read, "'Diversity' is a code word for #whitegenocide." Mindy and I both found the signs disturbing, and Mindy found them frightening. We wondered if we really wanted to stop in that little town for lunch. We did, partly because we were hungry and grumpy, partly because we didn't want to judge an entire town based on hateful billboards a few people ... maybe only one...put up. We ate at a charming diner on the historic courthouse square, but we couldn't help but wonder how many of the people we saw might be supportive of those racist signs.

We learned that in 2013 the community had a big controversy over a billboard that read "Anti-Racist is a Code Word for Anti-White." At that time the city issued a statement that read, "The mayor's office considers the content inflammatory, distasteful, and not in line with the truth on how Harrison is a city of welcoming and tolerant citizens." When we were there, everyone we saw in town seemed nice enough. Everyone we saw was also white, and we wondered if our treatment would have been different if either of us were a person of color.

***

We talked about issues of race with friends in Atlanta. Jerry and Keiko met in Japan when Jerry was a student there. They had gone to church with us in Healdsburg but had moved to Georgia when Jerry got a job there. Jerry said he was surprised by the distance between blacks and whites in the church. It seemed to him that blacks and whites were

twenty feet apart, and when a white person took a step, they were baffled that a black person wouldn't take a reciprocal step. He pointed out that when the white person's grandparent might have burnt a cross on the black person's grandparent's lawn, more than one step of reconciliation might be needed.

Easter morning we went to church with our friends. The congregation of this Presbyterian Church reflected the community in being primarily white people -- but there were a few African Americans, too I chatted with an elderly black woman in a yellow Easter dress and white hat. I asked her, as I often asked people, what brought her to this particular church.

She said she was there "by accident." I asked what she meant.

"It really wasn't an accident," she said, "God put me here." She's been at the church for a couple of years and even went on the church's trip to the Holy Land. She said that she still wasn't comfortable, but it seem to be the place God wanted her to be. It was, frankly, an odd conversation, but seemed to highlight the racial tensions still at play that an outsider might not see.

***

We heard about a church trying to address those tensions when we went to a bar in Atlanta, This bar was one of our favorites on the trip, maybe because it was a bar where people liked to play.

During my college years, Donkey Kong took an untold number of quarters that should have gone to laundry. At the Joystick Gamebar in Atlanta, Donkey Kong claimed another. There were plenty of other games available from back in the day: Space Invaders, Gauntlet, Defender, and Terminator pinball. The bar even had Dolly Parton pinball, which was new to us (we overheard one guy saying to another, with great sincerity, "It's not just pinball, it's Dolly Parton pinball.")

A shelf near the tables held a collection of board games, and other games were in use. We saw a couple playing Chutes and Ladders (and anyone who has raised small children knows this game, while not as bad as Candyland, is located on one of the mid-levels of Dante's Inferno, probably one involving gluttony or avarice).

A young white guy named Ben was taking on all comers for thumb wrestling. I foolishly volunteered and was ignominiously defeated. Ben was there with a group of friends from work for a farewell party. A chugging contest was another portion of the celebration, but I didn't join in.

I eventually got to talk to Ben and his friend Ross about bars and churches. Though they were young guys (late 20's) and neither attend church, they prefer their churches old -- Ben with the architecture and Ross with hymns and organs.

We also enjoyed chatting with Mary and Courtney, a black couple in their twenties, who told us about their dating life -- the good, the bad and the ugly of it (probably shouldn't get into too much of that here, but the stories involved stalking and cars being keyed). We asked what made for a good bar and Courtney said he likes good company and strong drinks with a heavy pour. Mary liked decent seats and tables with a place for your purse as well as your drink.

Before we could ask about churches, they needed to get in a quick game of foosball against another couple, but eventually they got back to us. Mary said she likes the music in a church to be upbeat; she mentioned Kirk Franklin and a choir. Courtney said he looks for entertainment in a church -- watching the strange person who's clapping offbeat and singing offkey. He tries to make babies cry. He told us he went forward for communion once and asked for a second wafer (he said he got a strange look, a shrug, and a second wafer).

Then we met a group who'd come to celebrate one friend, Lindsey's, thirtieth birthday. We asked the group our questions. Lindsey's husband, Dylan, likes a clean bar with no smoking. He said the Joystick has a small town atmosphere that's comfortable on weekdays, but is quite different on weekends. That's not when he wants to be there.

Lindsey said she looks for a church where the Gospel is preached. We loved that answer, because then we got to ask what she meant by the Gospel. She said, "That we sinners needed Christ to die for our sins." She said she appreciates that in a city that's ethnically diverse, like Atlanta, her church values bringing people of all races together.

Dylan's friend, Daniel, grew up in a very conservative church, and his dad was the pastor. When he was sixteen, his dad said he could go to whatever church he wanted, and he chose a less conservative Baptist church than the one his dad pastored. Daniel said Jesus wasn't judgmental, and churches shouldn't be either.

Daniel's girlfriend, Karen, said she believed the Church was changing, becoming "more modern" and less likely to judge people for, say, drinking in a bar. She said the city is changing too. "Atlanta is making me want to go to church again." Lindsey and Dylan told us more about their downtown church, Renovation, and we decided to visit to the Friday night service.

***

We certainly seemed to be among the oldest people in the crowd, which was composed primarily of millennials and whatever they call people in their thirties with kids. We joined the congregation in singing Mahalia Jackson's "Troubles of This World" with great soul and sadness -- if you can't sing the blues on Good Friday, when can you? We sang "Were You There?" in preparation for communion. (I was a little disappointed that we sang the final verse "Were you there when He rose up from the grave?" which really should be saved for Easter.)

One of the things I found intriguing about the church, expressed in their literature and at their website, was their goal of being "transcultural." They desire to bring about restoration between the blacks and whites of the city with a history of hostility. Leonce B. Crump Jr., the founding and lead pastor of the Centre City branch of Renovation is an African American. Justin Schaeffer, pastor of the Eastside Branch of Renovation, is white. The worship team includes people who appear to have a variety of racial backgrounds.

Sadly, Martin Luther King's quote about Sunday worship being the most segregated time of the week seemed to hold true for most congregations in Atlanta, but not for Renovation. They seek to build "a Jesus-Centered, Socially Conscious Transcultural Church." This church gave me hope that someday this will be true of the American Church as a whole.

5
APPALACHIA

There were places we planned to visit long before our adventure began, but most choices were made along the way -- sometimes on the spur of the moment. While we were wandering around the South, Mindy got a message from a friend: "If you don't have a church yet for North Carolina, you need to go the First Baptist Church in Franklin. They serve breakfast to hikers on the Trail."

Our friend Kira was talking about the Appalachian National Scenic Trail, which begins at Springer Mountain, Georgia, and ends 2,100 miles later at the top of Mount Katahdin in Maine. Most who plan to hike the whole route -- they're called "thru-hikers" -- go from South to North because that's how the weather works best.

Like many people, I hadn't been aware that hiking the Appalachian Trail was a thing until I read Bill Bryson's *A Walk in the Woods*, one of several literary inspirations for our trip. In his forties, Bryson took on the challenge of hiking the Trail and wrote a book which ended up being about his failure to complete his walk. (We hoped our trip wouldn't end up in that kind of book.) Kira (whose trail name was Lucky) planned to thru-hike, and we'd been following her posts, hoping to meet up with her sometime during the spring or summer.

Franklin, North Carolina, is near the hundred-mile mark from the southern end of the trail, and the town is an official Appalachian Trail community. The town hosts a trail day each year, and during March and April, hikers are a common sight in the motels and hostels (and laundromats). First Baptist Church began serving breakfast to hikers at the height of the season in 2008, and each year the number of people taking advantage of the free meal (and other benefits...more on that in a minute) grows.

We called the church to see if we could help with breakfast for a few days, and they assured us we'd be welcome. We arrived at 6:45 am, well before the sun was over the mountains, to find the kitchen full of workers manning half a dozen grills, some for pancakes and some for bacon. Others were setting napkins and plasticware around tables for eight throughout the basement dining room. Each table had a stack of envelopes and note paper along with pens and slips of paper with Bible verses on them.

Senior pastor Dr. Robert Brown, who was about our age and welcomed us warmly, invited me to ride along as he picked up hikers in one of the church vans. We drove to a local hostel, and a dozen waiting people filled the seats. On the five minute drive back to church, Robert asked where people were from; some from Virginia, Florida, and Pennsylvania. During the ride, I heard conversations about the joy of showers after a hundred miles on the trail -- and the importance of good footwear. We dropped everyone off, and the smell of bacon, coffee, and pancakes drifted out through the church door.

When we got back, Patsy, who runs the breakfasts (and works at the local Dollar Tree), welcomed hikers with the spiel she repeats each morning during the month-long season: "You can come up for seconds, thirds, and fourths -- we're not keeping track. If you leave here hungry, it's your fault, not ours. Today's menu is bacon and pancakes, but if you're taking a zero day [a rest day, when hikers catch up on laundry, shopping, and general cleanup before moving on], you're welcome to come back again, when the menu will be…" She paused, and returning guests joined her in saying, "Pancakes and bacon."

I joined the end of the food line. Three good sized pancakes were on my plate along with a healthy (unhealthy?) serving of bacon. A long table with butter and syrup, as well as pumpkin and apple butter and Mennonite raspberry jam, also had baskets of donated protein bars and cookies hikers could carry away with them. Coffee, tea, and orange juice were on another table.

Hikers need a lot of fuel, and most breakfast guests made frequent returns to the serving line. Some vegetarians wanted the flapjacks alone, but most hikers were thrilled by the bacon. Somebody said they dreamed of bacon on the trail, and the kitchen staff was happy to make their dreams come true. Some were excited about the orange juice ("No scurvy today!" one hiker chirped).

But the food wasn't all the church offered the hikers each morning. Mindy helped Connie, a short, motherly-looking volunteer, take digital photos of guests. While the hikers ate, Connie printed their pictures on photo paper and delivered them to the hikers by the time they finished their second (or third) plate of pancakes and bacon. I was reminded of the days of Polaroid -- especially because Mindy and Connie tended to wave the freshly printed photos as they wandered around the tables delivering them to the hikers.

You'd think that with cell phones people wouldn't care about mailing photos and notes home, but they did. Patsy told the hikers, "You've made it a hundred miles, and somebody wants to know that you're alive and getting a good meal." The church covered the postage on the notes, whether they were going to New Zealand, the Netherlands or even another part of North Carolina. Most hikers took advantage of access to the USPS, sometimes asking if they could get a second photo (often with a group) for another note. We even heard about a hiker who proposed marriage through a First Baptist Franklin letter.

Each year they've held the breakfast, the church made posters for the hikers to sign with their trail names. Previous years' posters hung around the room, and hikers looked for names they knew. The poster for 2016 already had an additional sheet of poster paper added, and it was looking full, too.

After a half hour or so of eating, note writing, and picture taking, Pastor Robert got everyone's attention when he said, "I'm going to talk for two minutes. You can time me." He read Hebrews 12: 1 & 2 and talked about running the good race and fixing our eyes on Jesus. He finished before his two minutes were up, and he later told me he has four short talks that he used in rotation for the three or four breakfast weeks. (We were only there for four breakfasts, one covered by associate pastor Jack Jarrett, so we didn't hear a repeat.)

I asked Robert about the people who walk the AT, especially the people who expect to hike the five or so months it takes to walk from Georgia to Maine. He said thru-hikers are often going through transitions in their lives: divorce, loss of a loved one, sometimes retirement. He'd had substantial conversations with many hikers, sometimes corresponding with them along the trail and after they finished their walk.

A couple in their sixties (I think his name was Lighthouse) came for breakfast all four mornings we were there, and Mindy sat with them while she had breakfast. For them, the hike was a physical and a spiritual challenge that they wanted to do while they could. The Trail ran near their son's home in Pennsylvania, and they thought they'd probably stop there, but until then, they were enjoying going slowly and meeting people along the way.

Another hiker had brought his violin along, and he played for all of us on the two mornings he came to breakfast. Others brought their dogs; one day at the laundromat we saw a hiker with his girlfriend and their dog. That morning she'd stayed at the hostel with the dog, assuming dogs wouldn't be welcome at the church, and he'd brought a plate back for her and their dog. All three were at breakfast the next day.

During the first breakfast, Patsy announced they'd reached 500 guests for the year so far, with only a week or so left in the season. By our fourth and final morning, over 700 meals had been served, and Patsy was able to make another special announcement: the city acknowledged the church for their work promoting Franklin as a destination on the A.T. and had donated a $500 check (so the church could "buy more bacon.")

Often I heard hikers thanking the servers. "You're angels," said one man. One woman thanked Patsy for the work the church did, and Patsy replied, "We as a church get much more than we give to you. The work of the breakfasts brings us together in the church as a community."

We came to greatly admire Patsy, who's involved in all kinds of service projects in the church and the community, and we were happy to get to visit her at work and stocked up on our regular Dollar Tree supplies (disposable razors, pretzels, Butterfinger bars).

The church has other ministries besides the breakfast. In a few weeks, the church would be sending a work team to serve a church in Honduras. They have Good News Clubs at local elementary schools, and we got to help at the Saturday Community Lunch (more pancakes and bacon!) where clothes and toiletries are free to those who need them. Still, the breakfast service was a unique ministry that the church could provide because of their location and willing volunteers. This week confirmed for us that churches should figure out what unique ministries they can contribute using their site and their resources.

After church in Franklin, we drove through Great Smoky Mountains National Park toward Tennessee. We stopped at the North

Carolina/Tennessee state line, where the Appalachian Trail crossed the highway, and we wondered how far away Lucky was. We walked along the trail for a few feet, hoping we'd happen upon her, but the wind was cold, and after a few photos of the view (and other AT hikers), we headed toward Tennessee.

***

In Nashville, we stayed with Craig, a high school friend of mine, and his wife Beckie in the rental unit they'd added to their home. When Craig first took Beckie to see the house, she'd refused to get out of the car. The building was run down, but the neighborhood was worse. Craig went to work on the house, and after a lot of work, it's a beautiful, comfortable home (with a great apartment above the garage).

The neighborhood, 12 South, has been rebuilt as well. You could probably describe it either as "renovated" or "gentrified," but we thought it was amazing. Reese Witherspoon opened a "brick and mortar for her new lifestyle brand Draper James" (I'm not sure what most of these words mean, but I found them at the website for her store). A bakery called the Five Daughters serves the best donuts I've ever tasted, and their website had a live feed so you could make sure your favorites were in stock. A food truck served nothing but custom s'mores. A cupcake shop had an ATM so you could buy a custom treat any time of the day or night. A paleta (Mexican popsicle) shop had a Baskin-Robbins range of flavors. And in that neighborhood, we had one of our most important bar conversations and heard one of our favorite church sermons.

***

Frankly, I was drawn to the bar by the sight of Golden State Warriors jerseys. The Warriors were on the verge of breaking the Chicago Bulls' record of most wins in a regular season, and I very much wanted to watch the game. My new Warrior friends and I were able to successfully root the Warriors on to a win. That wasn't the important thing, though.

We talked to a bartender that I'll call "Beth," and we found ourselves wondering if the whole trip had existed for the sake of that one conversation. Beth had cheerfully checked our I.D.s when we came in, which we always appreciate. Yeah, we know laws and policies in some places require bartenders to check everyone's I.D.s, but we still appreciate it; we can pretend that they just weren't sure about our age.

After a while, we asked our two questions, and she told us that a good bar has a sense of community and that it was more important to make a connection with the guest and to have a good conversation, rather than putting on a show. She said that a good church also has a sense of community, then she told us something about her background.

When she was a kid, she went to a Presbyterian Church. She said that not everyone was kind to her, but worshiping there spoke to her. She began to consider going into youth ministry someday. Around that time, her parents became Jehovah's Witnesses and wanted her to go to their church The church discouraged higher education, so she didn't pursue it. Youth ministry was no longer an option. She felt continually judged. She said, "A church should be your safe haven, your support system," but that isn't how she felt when she went to church with her parents.

She'd ended up as a bartender. She'd gone through hard times, and now her mother-in-law, a Southern Baptist who believed Beth was not worthy of her son, had stirred up conflict between them. Beth felt threatened by her husband and was considering a restraining order. Life was hellish.

While she was driving to work that evening, Beth said she'd thought about praying, "But I was afraid to pray. Because what if I prayed and there was no answer? That would mean God wasn't there, and I wouldn't have anything."

Before we'd chosen our bar for the evening, we'd prayed about where we should go, and asked God to guide us. We could assure Beth that God exists and that He cares about her. We said maybe God brought us that very night so we could pray for her. And we put Beth on on prayer list, committing to pray for her for the year to come. We don't know any more of her story, but she's still in our hearts.

***

A couple of days later, we walked a few blocks with Craig and Beckie to church. Not surprisingly (we were, after all, in Nashville) the musicians were excellent, though they played along the wall, rather than in front where they'd draw attention to themselves. The sermon was on Jonah, and the central theme was the danger of self-righteousness. Elliott Cherry (who was bearded, spectacled, and tattooed) preached. I heard Elliott called both an "interim pastor" and a "pastor in residence" for Midtown Fellowship's 12 South congregation, and he argued that the key to the whole book is found in Jonah's cry from the belly of the fish, "Salvation belongs to the Lord."

The great missionary to China, Hudson Taylor, did something groundbreaking in his time. He dressed like the Chinese around him to follow the Apostle Paul's example of being all things to all men. I don't know whether Elliott was trying to follow their example or not, but he looked like a hipster pastor to hipsters. He wore a purple and red plaid shirt, jeans, retro glasses, a full beard, and short hair, and his arms were visibly tattooed. The smug, condescending attitude often associated with hipsters was totally absent.

Elliott said our problem is believing that we can save ourselves -- which is another way to describe self-righteousness. Elliott called it "the grossest thing we are capable of" before giving five signs for identifying self-righteousness in ourselves ("Don't worry," he said, "This will get uncomfortable.").

> 1) We are not a comfort to hurting people.
> 2) Troubled people don't want to talk to us about their problems.
> 3) We feel perpetually worried and anxious (we think solving problems is up to us).
> 4) We're unable to receive criticism.
> 5) And the biggest sign of self-righteousness is not thinking we're self-righteous (because everyone is).

When I talked to him after the worship service, I said we'd talked to a lot of people in bars who feel the church is a place of judgment.

He said the biggest reason for the world's hatred of the church is self-righteousness. He'd heard someone say that the church would be better off if there were more sermons directed toward the older brother in the story of the Prodigal Son, rather than the younger. (In the Luke 15 story, the younger's sins center on depravity, while the older is self-righteous.) Elliot added, "We'd like to be known as a hospital for sinners, not a museum for saints."

***

We left Nashville after church with a promise to visit Beckie and Craig at their other home in West Virginia, where Craig ran a non-profit in one of the poorest counties in the state. But first, we needed to revisit a place from Mindy's past.

We enjoyed a variety of tourist sites in Kentucky: Mammoth Caves, Colonel Sanders' original kitchen, and Cumberland Falls (one of the only places, besides Victoria Falls in Zambia, where you can see a "moonbow" on clear full moon nights). Our primary destination, though, was a tiny community in the hollers of southeastern Kentucky. Mindy's home church in Indiana has brought high schoolers to work at Morris Fork Church since sometime in the late 1960s, usually doing repair projects and running a vacation Bible school.

When Mindy contacted the church, we were told we could stay in the Manse (the Presbyterian word for where the pastor lives. No pastor lives there now, but the name has stuck) and also that there would be projects waiting for us. After we arrived, Edie welcomed us and asked if we'd scrape and paint the ground floor of the manse to prepare it for summer visitors.

Morris Fork is remote but beautiful. Electricity, paved roads, and telephones didn't come to the area until the mid 20th century. The nearest grocery store is about an hour away (there's a convenience store in the next town, by the gas station, if fresh produce isn't a priority) Families in the hollers have lived there for generations.

Matt, a high school junior, painted with us on Saturday. We talked about science fiction novels and college possibilities. I asked what he liked about the area, and he said, "There are times here where I've been at church and looking out the window, and I've seen a deer come close. You can't see that many places."

Edie was our host for the week, along with her stepdaughter, Patty. Edie is on the church board, though she lives more than an hour away. She's in her early seventies, and she comes to Morris Fork about once a month to work very hard to keep the property up and to take care of Patty. Edie told us she'd asked God for help that week because she didn't know know how she'd get all the painting done. She said she believed we were an answer to her prayers. (About this time in the year we began to wonder if the project was about visiting bars and churches, or if in God's eyes the year was about things like painting a basement in Kentucky.)

***

"Are you a redneck or a hillbilly?" a little boy asked Beckie, our Nashville host, while she was walking her dog near their other home in McDowell County, West Virginia. She thought that was a somewhat limited range of choices, but choices have been limited in McDowell County for a long time now. Widely known as coal country, the area declined along with the industry throughout the middle of the last century.

In May, 1963, President John F. Kennedy said, "I don't think any American can be satisfied to find in McDowell County, in West Virginia 20 or 25 percent of the people of that county out of work, not for six weeks or 12 weeks, but for a year, two, three or four years." The county was a focus in Johnson's War on Poverty, but the area is still losing the war.

During the 1970's energy crisis, some hoped the area might flourish, but it didn't happen. In 1990, the poverty rate reached 37%, with half of all children in families below the poverty line. Since then, other industries had left, natural disasters such as floods have devastated the region, and human disasters such as drugs -- OxyContin has been particularly destructive -- continue.

With the reduced tax base, the educational system has suffered. Most young people see few options when they look to the future. Craig came to the area hoping to provide more options.

About a year before we visited, Craig incorporated the non-profit organization Warrior Creek Development (named for the creek that runs through the county). One of the organization's goals is to offer training and skills to young people; another is to provide suitable housing for teachers.

Through Warrior Creek's two year program, willing men or women work construction 33 hours each week, attend six hours of classes at Southern West Virginia Community and Technical College, and agree to three hours of life coaching. Those who complete the program will have an Associates degree in Applied Science in Construction, and, Craig hopes, a more balanced view of life. He tells prospective program members, "I want you to know I'm a follower of Jesus, but you don't have to be a Christian or become a Christian to be part of this program. I just think you should know my foundation for living so that it won't take you by surprise. I don't want that to be a Trojan Horse."

One of the many challenges faced by the education system of McDowell County was a lack of adequate housing for teachers. When we visited, Warrior Creek was building three structures designed to provide quality housing to attract new teachers to the area. Not long after we wrote about the project, one of those prospective teachers contacted us to let us know how excited they were for the opportunity to live and work in the area, and how much they appreciated knowing they'd have a good place to live.

In answer to the little boy's question, Beckie said she was a hillbilly. Craig and Beckie have committed to the hill country of McDowell County so that boy will have more options in his world.

6
HOMELESS IN THE CAPITAL

We'd set ourselves some arbitrary rules for the year. The primary, unbreakable rule (a church and a bar in every state) meant we needed to go to a worship service in every state and have a drink and chat with folks in some drinking establishment. Some rules, like not going to Applebees or Denny's, were more like guidelines. One important rule was spending at least one night in every state.

Before starting the trip, we'd decided to add the District of Columbia to the states. We knew we couldn't do Puerto Rico, Guam, Samoa, the North Mariana Islands, or the Virgin Islands (U.S.), but at least we could visit the nation's capital. We didn't know anyone who lived in the city of Washington proper, and Facebook shoutouts had yielded nothing. The District doesn't seem to have any campgrounds, and we thought pitching our tent by the Washington Monument might be frowned upon.

We researched hotels and found them to be not at all cheap, which made us sad because we are big fans of cheap -- as was our bank account. Apparently, ambassadors from Saudi Arabia and lobbyists for Monsanto have bigger travel budgets than we did. We entered Washington D.C. in travel websites with our budget numbers, and they'd send us to Virginia or Maryland.

So we decided to try something else. The monastery in D.C. required months of notice, and we needed a place right away. Mindy had read about an organization called CSM (City Service Mission) that organized student mission trips in urban areas and introduced pastors and leaders to the program by allowing them to stay overnight at their various sites before bringing youth. It seemed like a possible solution for us. We wanted to know about their work in Washington D.C., even though we weren't exactly their usual group. I called CSM headquarters in Philadelphia to ask if we could visit their Washington, D.C. ministry. Like the monastery, they needed a month's notice.

We decided we'd have to bite the bullet and pay big money for a motel in D.C. We figured at least we'd accumulate some points toward gold status on our Choice Hotels membership.

***

Since we were still curious about CSM's ministry in Washington, I called their office in D.C and left a message. The woman who returned the call said she'd be happy to give us a tour and directed us to their office in the basement of Douglas Memorial United Methodist Church. It was a three-story red brick edifice with tables of free produce outside. We went through the door to the child care center and downstairs to the CSM office.

Jessica, the CSM city director (and the woman on the phone), and Rachel, the assistant director, greeted us. Neither was over thirty, and they'd worked together at CSM Boston. They welcomed us and quickly began to interrogate us about our trip. It took some effort to get back to talking about their work in the nation's capital. We asked if there were any way we could help them, and Jessica said they needed some help the next morning, rearranging furniture to make room for the summer work team coming that weekend.

After they'd showed us around, Jessica asked where we were staying in D.C., and we said we didn't know, but we guessed we'd find a motel, though we couldn't afford it.

"Do you want to stay here?" she asked, and handed us a key, saying we could stay for the next three nights -- until their next group arrived on Friday. We were free to take our pick of the three rooms full of bunk beds, and we could store our food in one of the refrigerators in the kitchen. Once again, a gracious form of hospitality caught us by surprise. Jessica and Rachel made us feel at home in the big city.

Really, that's what CSM does as a ministry: make people feel at home in urban areas. CSM has ministries in ten other U.S. cities and Tijuana, Mexico. Churches send students, leaders, even families to CSM sites for an urban adventure. CSM sends people out to play with children who need care, serve meals to the hungry, make beds in rescue missions, and provide a wide variety of chores designed to make the lives of those in need a little better.

On CSM trips guests also can experience, in small ways, the lives of the poor. Teams go on an "urban plunge:" small groups are sent out for a set number of hours to fend for themselves with extremely limited cash and resources. If it rains or snows, gets cold or hot, the group must find shelter somewhere other than their CSM home.

Jessica told how she'd seen God work in the groups that have visited. When she was part of the ministry in Boston, a firefighter, a tough guy, came as the leader of a group. Jessica was terrified as he drove through Boston's streets like a firefighter, but when the week was over, he told her that the people he'd met, people in great need, could be the people he loved if they'd been born in different circumstances. The tough guy had grown in compassion.

***

Thousands of tourists come to Washington D.C. every year to see the monuments and tour the buildings. Rachel and Jessica and ministries like CSM show people a different part of the District of Columbia, but we still wanted to see the monuments. Both of us had been to the

National Mall in the 1970s when Mindy went with a school group, and I went with my family. We'd heard about the Vietnam Wall, the Korean War Memorial, and the World War II Memorial, and that first afternoon in Washington, we managed to see them, and they were as moving as we'd heard. But we were surprised to find a less permanent monument.

On 9/11/2015, a large structure called David's Tent was set up. Since then, it's usually, though not always, on the National Mall. For 24 hours every day, people worshiped God in that tent. We remembered the International House of Prayer (IHOP for short) near Kansas City, another place we'd visited where worship never stops.

Jason Hershey, who founded the David's Tent project, wrote, "Our desire is to call attention to the beauty of Jesus and to lead our generation in celebrating that Jesus is Lord. He should be enthroned above every area of our lives, even above the government of our great nation." The goals of the project are first to worship Christ, second to pray for the nation, and third to tell people about the good news of salvation found in Jesus. On their website, David's Tent claimed to be the longest-running outdoor worship event in U.S. History. As of June, 2018, worship continues, with a group from each of the US states leading worship for a week at a time.

When we found the tent, in the early afternoon, a young woman greeted us at the entrance. One man was playing guitar, and a half dozen people were joining him in praise. Since the tent looked like it could fit at least a hundred folks, it seemed woefully underpopulated. Sometimes that's what faithfulness looks like.

After praying for a moment, we left to see other landmarks in the National Mall, and then we drove to see a few buildings that represent the three branches of government. We saw the Capitol Building, the White House, and the entrance to the Supreme Court.

***

In spite of talk (and legislation) about the separation of church and state, a whole lot of church and faith issues have been decided by the Supreme Court in the last few years, and more will come. We took a particular interest in seeing the Supreme Court building because we spent time with an Arizona couple who'd had business there the year before.

In Phoenix, Arizona, Pastor Clyde Reed and his wife, Ann, met us for lunch at an Olive Garden Restaurant. I'd read about the Supreme Court case he'd been part of, and when I emailed him, he was happy to talk not just to us, but also to the wait staff.

When I'd contacted Clyde about getting together, he joked about enjoying the last gasps of their fading national fame. Through his career, Clyde alternated between jobs in churches and his other vocation, as an electrical engineer.

Before we talked about his case, though, Clyde had a question for Danny, who waited on our table. "Do you mind if I ask you a religious question?" Clyde definitely wasn't shy and retiring, which is good, considering the year before, members of the national media had interviewed him regarding the small church plant he'd served. Good News Presbyterian met in rented facilities in Gilbert, Arizona. It was important for the church to post signs to give the time and location of the Sunday morning services, and usually, those signs were posted on Friday nights and collected again on Sunday afternoon.

One Sunday afternoon, as he was collecting the signs, Clyde found a citation saying the signs were in violation of Gilbert city ordinances. At least one of the signs was confiscated. When Clyde went to city hall, he was told that church signs could be posted no more than two hours before the service and removed one hour after the service. Church signs also had to meet specific size regulations.

Clyde was puzzled. He'd seen signs for yard sales posted days before the event that remained for days after the event. He'd seen signs for candidates that were much larger than the regulations given for his signs. When he asked, officials told him that regulations for church signs were different than regulations for other signage.

At a loss as to how his congregation of forty to sixty people could afford to fight city hall, Clyde was surprised when a minister friend informed him about the Alliance Defending Freedom, a Christian non-profit organization primarily aids in the litigation of First Amendment issues. ADF took the case which became known as "Reed v. Town of Gilbert." The congregation was supportive of the legal course even when four consecutive decisions ruled for the city, against the church. When one justice out of four in the Ninth District ruled for the church, the case could proceed to the Supreme Court.

The ADF lawyers argued that by singling out churches for different signage rules, the city of Gilbert was discriminating against speech (in signs) because of its religious nature. The Supreme Court's ruling was unanimously in favor of the church.

When Danny came back with our food, she had an answer for Clyde's religious question, "Suppose that you were to die today and stand before God, and He were to say to you, 'Why should I let you into my heaven?' What would you say?"

She said if she went to Heaven, God would say, "I'm glad to see you!" In return visits to the table, Danny and Clyde continued their conversation. Before we left, Clyde encouraged Danny to visit Good News Presbyterian, even though he'd retired and wasn't pastoring anymore.

When Clyde stepped away from the table at one point, his wife Ann confided that she was always a bit afraid that if Clyde died before she did, the Cloak of the Evangelist, like Elijah's cloak on Elisha, would pass to her. Clyde wears the cloak well; he's very persuasive, and I'm glad that his lawyers in the Court were as well.

**

Almost everyone in the United States agrees that the separation of church and state is a good thing, but people don't agree where that line of separation should be. Sometimes that line is rather blurry.

The National Cathedral -- or, as it's properly known, The Cathedral Church of Saint Peter and Saint Paul of the City and Diocese of Washington --was built very close to that blurry line.

Because the District of Columbia was wholly ruled by Congress back in the day, that legislative body passed a charter in 1893 that allowed the Episcopal Church to build a cathedral in D.C.

In 1907, President Theodore Roosevelt saw the cornerstone laid, and when the final finial (decorative piece) was put in place, President George H. W. Bush was there. The United States Congress designated the Cathedral as "the National House of Prayer."

Three Presidential funerals (Eisenhower, Reagan, and Ford) were held in the Cathedral. Inaugural prayer services for five Presidents (FDR, Reagan, both Bushes, and Obama) were held there as well. I found myself asking, was the place built to honor God or the country?

Inside the Cathedral, near the choir loft and behind the pulpit and lectern (the "apse"), there's a seat for the bishop of the diocese. The chair indicates the church is the home church of the presiding bishop; it's called a "cathedra," and it's what makes a church a cathedral in the Episcopal Church. But at the back of the church, near the entrance, there's a statue of Abraham Lincoln. For the last century (at least) there's been a debate about Lincoln's Christian faith, and yet he is a prominent figure throughout the Cathedral.

In one of the many chapels, cushions on the seats honor a great variety of Americans, from Gerald Ford to Jefferson Davis, Harriet Tubman to Jane Adams, Wilbur Wright to Horace Greeley. These are persons of note, but should they be honored in a church? (Since the musical came out, there seems to be widespread agreement that Alexander Hamilton should be honored everywhere, so nobody seems to question his cushion's presence.)

Lenelle, an acquaintance of Mindy's from grad school days, led our tour group through the National Cathedral, and she mentioned a bit of controversy on the issue of Church v. State in the 1970's. The Nixon administration didn't believe that a moon rock, brought to earth through millions of taxpayer dollars, belonged in a church window, even the beautiful window where the rock was placed. Since the window (and the rock) are still there, maybe a higher power than Tricky Dick felt differently.

As we watched the school tour groups wander the pews, it was hard to remember this was a place of worship. But at 10:30 am, an amplified voice asked for a moment of silence, followed by a prayer from a priest. Lenelle had told us that the National Cathedral had been her church for several years, and she said she appreciated these occasional reminders that the place isn't just a tourist attraction.

Sunday morning worship is the best attended Episcopal service in the diocese, with about 1,500 people, but we were there on Thursday at noon for worship in the Bethlehem Chapel along with fifteen others. There was no music, and we followed the order of worship in the Book of Common Prayer. There was nothing patriotic about it.

When wars ended, people of a variety of faiths gave thanks in the Cathedral. When Martin Luther King Jr. or Billy Graham or the Dalai Lama needed a pulpit, the National Cathedral provided it. When the nation mourned after 9/11, the Cathedral provided a place to remember the victims. Finding the proper Church/State divide was a challenge, but as I remembered times the nation needed to work together to deal with spiritual issues, I was grateful the Cathedral straddled that line.

***

Since matters of Church and State were never far from our minds, if only because the working title for our project was "Church and States," when we found a bar called Church and State a few blocks from Douglas Memorial while we were staying there, we had to visit.

We were tempted (okay, I was tempted) by the downstairs bar in the same building, which had a video game theme (both bars had the same owners), but we climbed to the second floor and found stained glass and pews dominated the decor, with a separate room called Pastor's Study.

The menu, which looked like an old-timey newspaper called *The Church & State Times*, emphasized the "State" element. The preamble read, "This is not a Church. D.C. is not a State. But every bottle, whether heavenly or devilish, comes from the United States, its territories and possessions. We are the first all-American cocktail venue. Our craft cocktails take time, we appreciate your patience and invite you to be free and brave."

I'd never before read a menu I felt obliged to salute. Only real American spirits (no vodka here), and we ordered American drinks, a Jack Rose for me and a Mint Julep for Mindy. (The menu also had a church side, with "Seven Deadly Sins" and "Hymns" selections.)

Our bartender Victoria, like many Washingtonians, was involved in politics, with a full-time job in the District, working for what she called a "white hat cause." She considered bartending a creative outlet, "another skill that will help in the long run" where she could have short conversations with a variety of people. We doubted she wore her sleeveless leopard print top when lobbying, though. She said she liked a bar to be "a little sexy, a little seductive," but for locals, she likes her bar to be known for that "*Cheers* atmosphere." Community in church, she said, is a good thing, but she wanted a degree of anonymity along with it to avoid "people judging and everybody getting in everybody's business."

Her remark about bad experiences in churches made me think of something we heard in a church in Tucson, Arizona, "When people have a bad experience in a bar, they go down the street to another bar. When people have a bad experience in a church, they quit going to any church for years."

In researching our posts, we found an article in the Daily Beast that listed the District of Columbia as the nation's second drunkest state" (while acknowledging the District isn't a state) based on the number of drinks consumed by adults and the percentage of the population classified as binge and heavy drinkers (using information from the Center for Disease Control). The District was in the bottom five (again, among states) in a Gallup poll of church attendance. We appreciated that Church and State was designed to provide an experience people would remember rather than drinks to help them forget.

***

For us, the most encouraging experience in Washington D.C. was at the movies. We'd seen trailers for *Sing Street* and were happy to find it playing at Landmark E Street Theater. We arrived on a rainy evening to find a table set up with information about a film about human trafficking called *The Abolitionists*.

A lot of people were scurrying around to set up tables and food trays for an event. We had time before our film started, so we asked an event organizer a few questions. She told us some government officials would be coming to the screening -- Senator Orrin Hatch was rumored to be among them. The woman we were talking to, like me, had spent time working in youth ministry. She mentioned that she was a Latter Day Saint, and said the production of the film was sponsored by the Mormon Church, which hoped to bring about legislation to protect the thousands of women and children trapped in the modern slave market.

In Nevada, you saw gambling of some kind everywhere you went. In the District of Columbia, it seemed there was always lobbying of some sort, even in a theater lobby. But this looked like good lobbying to us.

As positive as that interaction was, what truly inspired us that night was *Sing Street*. It tells the story of a young man attending a Catholic school in Ireland in the 1980's, a time of economic woe for the country.

Conor, the protagonist, seems to have few options for joy in his life, but he decides to start a band to impress a girl. Writer and director John Carney, based the film (to some extent) on his own life.

During our trip, there were many times when I wondered if we were fools for going on this venture. After all, most people don't quit their jobs and hit the road. At the end of the movie, Conor and Raphina set off on their adventure knowing they may never get the chance again. A huge wave hits the boat, threatening to capsize it, and they laugh. The adventure is worth any risk.

I sat in the theater as the credits rolled, wiping the tears from my cheeks. The film captured the joyful senselessness of some of life's best adventures. As one of the film's songs advises, sometimes you've got to "drive it like you stole it."

7

SLEEPING IN THE MINIVAN

For years, Mindy argued that she was five feet, two-and-three-quarters inches (she'd given up on being taller than her mother, who was 5'3", but she didn't want to be the same height). Now she's secure enough to admit that she is perhaps 5'2". I'm 6'3". At our wedding, people laughed because I had to lean down to kiss Mindy, while she stood on tiptoes. When we met, she believed short women shouldn't date tall men because it wasn't fair to tall women. She allowed an exception to that rule after we started dating.

I bring this up because our heights made a difference when we slept in the van. Mindy could stretch out across one of the back seats much better than I could. She actually claimed to be comfortable sleeping on the shorter middle seat.

As we planned the trip, we hoped the majority of nights would be spent in the homes of friends and relatives. We brought our tent and sleeping bags along, figuring that we'd spend plenty of nights in campgrounds, and we knew that hotels (well, motels) would be an occasional necessity, but our bank account put serious limits on that option. Nights in the van didn't seem like a real option (especially when we saw how much space our belongings used).

Until Delaware. Like many people, we had our doubts that Delaware actually existed. We even left it off our planning lists (accidentally), which meant we forgot to research friends and churches in the area ahead of time, and we didn't know anyone.

***

At a church potluck in Newark, I asked a woman, "What is there to do in Delaware? What should we see?" She thought for a moment and

said, "The Longwood Gardens are beautiful... Oh, but that's in Pennsylvania. You really should see...Oh, that's in Baltimore. Well, you can drive to many wonderful places from Delaware."

We ended up in Newark because, thanks to Claudia and Shimon, we had a place to stay from Monday through Thursday. Mindy and Claudia have been friends since junior high, and we'd enjoyed staying and worshiping with them in Maryland (Claudia had gotten us in contact with Lenelle at the National Cathedral, too, and had come into D.C. in order to tour it with us).

Shimon overwhelmed us when he used his travel points to arrange our stay at the Marriott Residence Inn in Newark. He apologized because he couldn't extend the stay through the weekend (we needed to be in town Friday and Saturday nights because, you know, church). We assured him we'd find someplace to stay.

The place Shimon got for us was much nicer than our usual Econo Lodge. Mindy had set $50 per night as our goal for lodging, and the Residence Inn would have been way out of our range. Our suite had a full kitchen, sitting room, and a bedroom Every morning, we could go to the reception area for a free breakfast with fresh fruit, eggs, cereals, breads, and breakfast meats. One night they even offered a free barbeque dinner.

***

The location turned out to be better even than the accomodations. I went for a walk on our first day in Newark and came across the mission of the Little Sisters of the Poor. When we'd been at church with Claudia and Shimon, a couple of Little Sisters had spoken about their ministry, and it was fun to come across them again so soon. I decided to stop by the next morning to see if there was any way we could help out, and if, since they work with the poor, they might have suggestions about where a couple of poor wayfaring strangers could spend Friday and Saturday nights.

The next day, I walked over again while Mindy stayed behind to work on blogs and tried to find someplace to stay for the weekend.

At Little Sisters headquarters, I asked the receptionist if I could talk to someone about the ministry, and I mentioned that Mindy and I would love to do some volunteer work during the week. She seemed a little baffled by the request, but asked me to wait (I was in a waiting room, after all) while she made some calls to find out who I should talk to.

I entertained myself while I waited by looking at posters and brochures that told the story of Jeanne Jugan, who grew up in extreme poverty in France following the Revolution. After years if working as a kitchen maid and a nurse, at 47, she welcomed an old, blind woman into her home. Soon she welcomed a second and a third. She raised money and brought in workers to help. The Order was formally established in 1839 and by the time of Jugan's death in 1879, over two thousand Little Sisters of the Poor served the indigent. Today the Order serves in 30 countries around the world, and in the state of Delaware.

Eventually a woman who didn't seem to be a nun came out and greeted me, offering to take me on a brief tour of the public areas of the Jeanne Jugan Residence, where elderly and indigent folk are cared for. She pointed out apartments where the residents are, for the most part, able to care for themselves, though they can't afford an independent place of their own. We looked around the residents' general store, which has groceries and other day-to-day essentials. She showed me the library and a coffee room, but she told me we couldn't go through the doors into the part of the residence housing those with a need for more care.

After the tour, my guide and I sat at a table by a glass wall overlooking the lawns and a garden area. She told me that most of the work on the ground was done by volunteers, and that some of those volunteers were also residents. Ten nuns and three priests live and serve the facility, providing rosary services, prayer meetings, Bible studies, and daily Mass. Religious services aren't mandatory, though, and being a Catholic is not a requirement to become a resident.

I asked whether Mindy and I could volunteer in any way while we were in town. She said her husband, who volunteered in the garden, was going to direct a group of students working on Saturday. She said maybe we could help then, and that she'd get back to us.

I sensed wariness about letting us help out, and I wondered how much was caution about having strangers around residents. I also wondered if contemporary politics had anything to do with her hesitation.

The Little Sisters of the Poor had been in the news around that time because of court disputes about requirements to pay for birth control and abortion-inducing drugs. And I came in saying we were writers, and it's always safe to be suspicious of writers.

We got a call the next day -- since there wasn't time to do a background check on us, we wouldn't have a chance to help out. I was glad I'd gotten to see the beautiful property and to hear about the good work they seemed to be doing, but I wished we could have seen more.

***

While I was learning about the Little Sisters, Mindy discovered that we'd arrived just in time for graduation at the University of Delaware. Everyplace -- motel, hotel, or campground -- in a 20 mile radius was booked.

She'd been doing some other research as well, and she'd found out about "stealth camping." She thought we could park the minivan in a parking lot or on a residential street late in the evening, spend the night, and leave before people were up. From what she'd read, it was edgy, but not illegal or dangerous. We'd also noticed a large truck stop/rest area nearby that looked clean and safe.

We agreed to think about the possibility, but we hoped we'd find another option. I hoped something else would turn up.

***

When we told people we were going to churches and bars they'd often joke, "Do you go to one right after the other?" Delaware was one of the rare places where we did. On Wednesday, we were welcomed and warmly included at Newark Christian Church's prayer meeting. Afterwards, we drove a few blocks to Hutch's Pub, where we were welcomed and watched a pool tournament (we even considered returning the next afternoon for dinner). Nobody at either place offered us a place to stay, and we didn't want to ask.

As we checked out of the Residence Inn on Friday, we still didn't know where we'd be sleeping. After an afternoon at the library and the mall, we pulled into a supermarket parking lot and watched *Clean and Sober* with Michael Keaton on Mindy's phone. (There weren't many choices for films set or filmed in Delaware, possibly because people didn't believe the state existed.)

It was dark when the movie ended, and we started looking for a place to park the van for the night. We drove through some neighborhoods looking for a spot that was away from houses and street lights, but nothing looked right. Besides, I really didn't like the idea of staying in a residential area, because I knew it would creep me out if people were sleeping in their vehicle in front of my house.

Around midnight, we pulled into the parking lot of the Newark Christian Church. We figured that at least people there knew us. We could have -- should have -- asked permission first, but we were embarrassed. Asking friends for someplace to sleep was bad enough. Asking total strangers seemed pathetic. Instead, we parked on the side of the church farthest from houses, with a couple of large, lidded plastic cups to deal with biological imperatives.

It didn't take long to move everything off the middle and back bench seats to the driver's and shotgun seats. With a suitcase under her head and some random luggage at her feet, Mindy was able to stretch out fully in the middle seat. I took the backseat, which was a little longer. I still had to curl up.

We cracked open one of the front windows and the rear vents. We expected the mid-May night to stay relatively warm, but we each had a sleeping bag and decided that sleeping in our clothes was more practical than trying to change.

The spot had seemed reasonably dark as we got settled, but after about ten minutes, a light on the side of the church flashed on for a minute, and then went off again. I figured it was a motion sensitive light that a cat or a squirrel had set off. But no. All night, that light turned on, then off, about every ten minutes.

Neither Mindy or I fell asleep quickly. We'd close our eyes, but after awhile, we'd pull out our tablets and read for awhile, then we'd doze for awhile. Eventually, the sky got a little lighter, and Mindy checked her phone to find out when the nearest Dunkin' Donuts, the one by Hutch's Pub, opened. To our delight, it had opened at 5:00 am, a few minutes earlier. We drove over; Mindy was happy for the coffee, I was happy for the donuts, and we both appreciated the Wifi.

***

It was Saturday morning, and we didn't want to spend another night at the church. While lingering over Mindy's coffee and our donuts, we decided to visit historical sites in New Castle. We learned that Delaware was created primarily so William Penn would have a place to land ships. We also saw several interesting churches and graveyards. By late afternoon, we were more than ready to see something built more recently, and we headed back to Newark for the Saturday services at The Journey.

Perhaps because we'd done without the night before, I was fascinated by the men's restroom at The Journey (Real Church for Real People), the only church we visited that had TVs over the urinals, all tuned to ESPN.

I asked Dave Jackson (his staff position is "Gathering Director") about this. He said the church specifically aims to creatively appeal to men between 20 and 40. I asked why young men were the target, and Dave said church growth statistics show that if you draw young men, young women and young families will follow, but that if you appeal primarily to women, men won't necessarily follow.

The church's sermon series are guy friendly. We were there for the final sermon in the "Limited Edition" series about our limitations as people, with a visual theme involving cars and racing. The cafe was decorated with racing flags and Rascal Flatts' "Life is a Highway" was playing overhead. Before the sermon there was a short video stealing freely from *The Fast and the Furious* franchise. Dave told us that a previous sermon series had a zombie apocalypse theme; the upcoming series was based on *The Godfather*.

Journey has two services on Saturday, and the 4:30 pm service had a number of theatrical aspects. The real theater, though, started during the second Saturday service. Just as the sermon began, the fire alarm lights flashed and a robotic, vaguely feminine voice repeated, "There is a fire emergency in the building. Please leave through the nearest exit."

What I found interesting was that at first, people weren't sure if it was a real fire alarm or part of the service. People started moving toward the exits, but more than once, we overheard, "I thought it was part of the sermon." Mindy and I agreed that it was a good thing when people expect to be surprised in a church. (I know expecting to be surprised is a bit of a contradiction)

Everyone in the building, even the kids' classes, evacuated to the parking lot. We couldn't see or smell any smoke, but disobeying the robot voice didn't seem like a good idea. Pastor Mark Johnston apologized to the congregation. He said there was no fire. The alarm system had malfunctioned, shutting off the power to the building. Since it would take a couple hours for everything to power back up, the rest of the worship service was canceled (when encouraged to preach the rest of his sermon from the loading dock in the parking lot, Mark said he wouldn't have any voice left for Sunday morning). Everyone was encouraged to come back the next day for one of the other three services.

As we got back into the minivan, Mindy and I looked around the parking lot and wondered out loud, "Should we stay here tonight?"

Before taking that step, though, we had another possibility to check out.

***

Usually we tried to avoid tollways, but that night we took the JFK Memorial Highway to the Delaware Welcome Center located right in the median area of the toll road. It was clean and bright, and inside, we found an Auntie Anne's Pretzels, a Popeye's Fried Chicken, a Burger King, a Starbucks, and even better, free Wifi. Best of all, there were restrooms, and the building (though not all of the businesses) was open all night long, so if we woke up and wanted to go, we could. After the night before it seemed like a miracle.

The parking lot lights were fairly bright, but we couldn't hear the trucks idling in another lot on the other side of the Welcome Center. We pulled our sleeping bags over our heads and slept soundly for least five hours or so, which was enough. After we cleaned up a little (and changed our clothes) in those miraculous Welcome Center restrooms, we took the next exit back to Newark Church of Christ for an outdoor worship service and barbecue potluck -- the same potluck where we heard about the places we easily drive to from Delaware..

The University of Delaware Fightin' Blue Hens had finished their graduations, and we found a cheap motel not too far from the Christiana Mall. Bed -- and showers -- felt so good.

***

After a quick tour of Longwood Gardens with our nephew, we headed towards Lancaster County. The area has some of the best place names in the United States, and I saw one of my favorite sights ever in the town of Intercourse. We'd stopped at a little pretzel shop staffed by two young women wearing white caps and long dresses. Mindy asked the women about the differences between their head coverings and we learned that one woman was Mennonite, and the other was Amish.

While we waited for the pretzels to cook, the Mennonite woman was shopping for a car on her phone and asking the Amish woman for her opinion. "Oh, that one's cute," we heard one say to the other -- which was a memorable moment, but it's not the most memorable picture we took away from our stop that day.

We sat on the shop's front porch to eat our fresh, warm pretzels, looking across the road at the National Penn bank branch, which had a drive-through window. We looked up to see an Amish woman drive her buggy away from the window after finishing her banking. Once again, we laughed, amazed at the opportunity to see such marvelous things.

***

Though we had a number of friends in the Philadelphia area, we hadn't figured out where we'd go to church -- which usually determined where we'd spend most of our time in a state. We spent a day and night near Hershey, taking the free factory tour and spending time with old friends who'd been urban missionaries in Indianapolis when Mindy was in high school. A California friend met us for dinner in Philadelphia (where we also visited a variety of historical sites -- or at least their gift shops -- and the steps of the art museum).

We went to another unique Pennsylvania site for the week's movie theater, and the bat flying around just added to the atmosphere. It was Fright Night at Colonial Theatre in Phoenixville, which has a long history of horror, science fiction, and the supernatural. Way back in the day, Houdini himself performed in the theater; most famously, the theater was used as a location for 1957's science fiction classic, *The Blob*. In that film, Steve McQueen played a teenager trying to convince the town that a monster from outer space was on the attack, and the town is convinced only when the amorphous extraterrestrial sends teens screaming from the theater. The film we saw that night, though, was *Carrie,* a film which depicts Carrie's fundamentalist mother as a dangerous loony toon.

***

We still hadn't found a church, though, until -- after several very restful nights with friends and at motels, we spent the night at a truck stop. We'd arrived late in the evening at a Flying J outside of Harrisburg and found a relatively dark spot to park (though we could hear diesel engines running through the night). In the morning, we looked out our windows and saw a sign that to us seemed both material (it was lettering on the side of a truck) and supernatural (read on).

The side of the truck parked about fifty feet away read, "Mobile Chapel Transport for Christ". We realized we had our church for the week. We'd never heard of the organization, but we knew we needed to learn more. During that week, we visited three chapels at different truck stops in Pennsylvania (and saw another at a church festival). Saturday night we slept at the Wilco Travel Plaza outside Harrisburg, and on Sunday morning, we met Chaplain Chris.

The chapel looks like a regular truck on the outside, but the inside looks more like a a modified mobile home with wood panelling and industrial-type carpeting on the floor. The walls were decorated with crosses, maps, and pictures of Jesus; near the door was a rack of brochures and flyers. Rows of chairs filled up much of the space in preparation for the day's worship services.

Chris, like most Transport for Christ chaplains, used to be a truck driver, but health concerns took him out of the business. We guessed he was in his early to mid forties, and he told us he was working on a counseling degree in order to more effectively minister to truckers who drop in. We weren't surprised when he told us that loneliness is a big issue for truckers. Marriages and family sometimes suffered when a driver was on the road for weeks at a time.

Stress, Chris told us, takes its toll on drivers, but when they come in a Transport for Christ Chapel, they rarely begin a conversation with the things that bother them most. Drivers will chat for half an hour before that bringing up what really bothers them, but then they often pour out their souls.

We learned that truck stop owners and managers often welcome chapels for their help in reducing incidents of drug dealing and prostitution, and in recent years chaplains have become alert to the dangers of human trafficking. Chris told us about another chaplain's experience at that very site.

A North Carolina woman was desperate to see her children, who lived with their father in Philadelphia. Commercial truck drivers can't legally carry riders, but the driver who offered the woman a ride soon made it clear that legalities weren't his strong suit. Instead of taking the woman to Philadelphia, he stopped outside Harrisburg and imprisoned her in his truck.

After three days, he left the woman alone in the cab of his truck while he went inside to eat at the Perkins'. The woman spotted the Transport for Christ mobile chapel and made a dash for it.

The chaplain welcomed her, and when the driver tried to follow her into the chapel, the chaplain turned him away and called the police. The woman refused to press charges, saying she just wanted to go home. A woman driver, a Christian, happened to stop by the chapel, and happened to have just completed her run. She was heading back to North Carolina, to the very place where the abducted woman wanted to go. The driver got her company's permission to give the woman a ride home. Only about 5% of truck drivers are women, and who knows what small percentage of those drivers live in North Carolina. It's not surprising that Chaplain Chris believed God took an interest in the matter.

All told, we slept in the van three nights that week. After that, it became part of our routine to spend a night or two in parking lots, and it wasn't long before Walmart became our favorite van-camping location.

Generally, we could find a dark, quiet, safe parking space. Most stores had strong Wifi (sometimes even good enough for streaming), which we appreciated because we had blog posts almost every day. The French bread from the bakery, especially the "everything" bread, was cheap but felt like a treat (and one loaf usually lasted us a couple of days). Still, the best thing about Walmart was that even when we climbed out of the minivan with rank breath, hair askew, and rumpled clothing, we fit in with the other middle-of-the-night Walmart shoppers.

8
LIFE WITHOUT THE MINIVAN

"Crack!"

Unless you're talking breakfast cereals, and the sound is accompanied by "snap" and "pop," this was not a good sound to hear in the middle of the night in a motel on Long Island. Mindy's foot had just come down on something, and she knew the sound was bad.

With the light on, she realized she'd stepped on our laptop, and the screen was hopelessly cracked. We were worried. Like the minivan, a computer was essential to life and work on the road. We used that laptop for writing our three blogs (Dean and Mindy go to Church, Dean and Mindy Walk into a Bar, and Movie Churches), and most of our photos were stored on it. We had to replace it, but we didn't think we could find the money in the budget. Not that there actually was a budget, just a quickly draining bank account and significant expenses coming in the next few weeks.

In the morning, we discussed responsibility: did the blame lie with the person who stepped on the computer, or on the person who left the laptop on the floor by the window? We examined the issue calmly...no wait. It was more "Let's not discuss this because it can't be helped, but I feel a simmering resentment against your thoughtlessness." At least we agreed.

We called tech daughter Paige, who suggested we could probably get by with a Chromebook costing a couple hundred dollars. We found what we needed at a Best Buy a few miles away, bought it and a hard drive, and with the help of the Geek Squad were able to post again. The death of the computer wouldn't end the trip, but we realized that something else might.

What would do it? The death of our car? An empty bank account? Sudden illness or injury?

***

Throughout the year, we told people we'd be going to a church and a bar in every state. A typical response was, "Even Alaska and Hawaii?" We assured them that the 49th and 50th state are indeed states, and included in the phrase "every state." Sometimes we'd elaborate, explaining that each year has 52 weeks, so we could visit all 50 states, plus Washington D.C., with a week to spare. Then they'd start asking if we'd be visiting Guam, too.

Anyway, at the conclusion of our week in New York (we drove up the Hudson with Jil, our Brooklyn daughter, visited a church and a bar on Staten Island, and broke our laptop on Long Island. It was an eventful week), we left the minivan with Mindy's college roommate, Carrie, and flew to Seattle.

Seattle daughter Paige and her husband, Grant, met us at SeaTac airport. They took us out to Buffalo Wild Wings, put our Hawaii bags in the trunk of their car, and took us back to the airport where, a few hours later, we flew out on Alaska Airlines. (Friends had asked about driving to Alaska, but weather and time elements prevented us. Besides, with all due respect to Canada, we wanted to spend the whole year in the US of A)

We arrived in Fairbanks, less than two hundred miles south of the Arctic Circle, around 2:00 am. The rental car place was closed, but our friend Stephen's parents picked us up and drove us to his house, which he was loaning us for our four-day stay. As we drove, it was plenty light enough to see people jogging, even a couple of kids riding their bikes. We'd purposely scheduled our visit near the summer solstice so we could see the legendary long summer days, but the twilight was weird. Not quite daylight, but definitely not dark. Still, we had no trouble getting to sleep once we got to Stephen's Winter Lodge.

We got up around 7:00 the next morning to a warm, beautiful day, and mid-morning, our friends took us back to the airport to pick up our rental car. That afternoon, we drove ten miles south to North Pole (not THE North Pole. North Pole, Alaska) where we mailed off a few postcards and visited a few of the Santa Claus related tourist spots.

We enjoyed the weird, extended days. Stephen invited us to his softball game, which started at 9:00 pm and ended around 10:30. No lights were needed, and other teams played later. After his game ended, we headed into town to visit our Alaska bar, but the late-afternoon light and warmth made it hard to believe it was after 11:00 pm.

***

Mecca Bar is a gathering place not only for Fairbanks people but for people who come to the second-largest city in Alaska from towns and villages for more than a hundred miles around. Mecca has hosted fundraisers, weddings, and memorial services.

Four days before we got there, events at Mecca got a little less smoky. Even though cigarettes are still for sale behind the bar, patrons had voted overwhelmingly in favor of banning smoking inside. Serena, the bartender, said, "It could get really bad in here, especially on the days when it gets 40 below outside" and doors and windows have to be kept closed. We didn't ask what smokers would do when winter came again.

The night we visited, the temperature was in the low seventies. In spite of the smoking ban, a lot of things at Mecca haven't changed much over the years. There's still a pay phone on the wall, and the mirrors on the ceiling and behind the bar have probably been there since the 1960s. At least two movies have featured the bar, 1979's *Spirit of the Wind* and 2007's *Into the Wild*.

When we sat down at the bar, half a dozen other people were already there, with more surrounding the pool table. I struck up a conversation with Merritt, a guy from Homer, Alaska. He was a boilermaker, a welder who worked on a variety of energy projects -- "It's not just a drink," he said. Part of the year, though, he's a crab fisherman, and he said he'd worked on the Cape Caution, a boat featured on the television show, *The Deadliest Catch*.

Merritt said that a good bar needed "socialism. But not the kind like communism, but the kind where people are sociable." He acknowledged the staff was also important, praising our bartender, Serena. He said that a good church came down to "the force of people." If the people are good, it is a good church.

Right then, an alarm interrupted the conversation. Someone had tried to open the emergency door at the back, in spite of signs that read "Emergency Exit" and "Not a Restroom." A bigger sign on the door says, "Pull." Serena hurried to turn the alarm off, and we heard the alarm goes off regularly.

Another guy at the bar, Andrew, had briefer answers to our two questions. For a good bar, he said, "Alcohol helps." When I asked what made a good church, he said, "I'm an agnostic." (Merritt said Andrew wasn't really an agnostic. I can't judge. Well, I can judge some things. Like sermons and hard ciders and the top ten episodes of the original *Star Trek*. But not this.)

While I was talking to Andrew and Merritt, Mindy was asking Serena our questions. She said she thought a good bar was "more the community. I work at two completely different bars. A bar can't function without people willing to come back. The Mecca's survived because of the community." (Other people mentioned family and community events they'd attended at The Mecca.)

Serena went on, "At church, you leave all your problems at the door. It's the same at a bar. Bars and churches both function as places of escape and support."

We were thinking about paying our tab and heading back to Winter Lodge when Serena said, "Somebody bought you a shot. Do you want it? It's a Duck Fart."

Andrew the Agnostic had bought a round of the layered Kahlua, Bailey's and Crown Royal shots for everyone at the bar. Serena passed around the glasses, and Andrew raised his with the toast, "To Alaska!" Everyone drank (it was delicious), we paid up and walked out into the sunny Alaska night.

***

An interesting factoid about Alaska is its consistent place toward the bottom in polls about church attendance in the United States. I asked Gary Cox, Pastor of University Baptist Church in Fairbanks (our friend Stephen's church) about this, and he said, "There's not a cultural tradition of church attendance as there is in the South. It's not the expected thing to do. People in Alaska have a fiercely independent spirit. There are many atheists and agnostics."

On the plus side, that means that people who attend church in Alaska want to be there. Especially when the temperature hits 40 below outside, and people could stay home on their warm comfy couches, it's encouraging to realize that everyone in the pews on those mornings considers church a high priority. I asked whether church attendance was lower in summer or winter, and Pastor Cox said people were more likely to stay away in summer. They want to enjoy the outdoors while they can on a beautiful (long!) summer days.

We figured we were raising the average local church attendance while we were there -- we attended University Baptist on Sunday morning, but we also went to the Seventh Day Adventist Church of Fairbanks on Saturday.

We'd only been at the Adventist church a few minutes before we were invited to stay for the visitors' lunch after the service, and we realized we weren't the only visitors. Two dozen others from Canada and the lower forty-eight were also worshiping at the Adventist church that morning.

Alaskans may be fiercely independent, but as we'd heard in the bar, that didn't keep people from expressing their need for community. During the service we heard about a health clinic in Fiji (which probably sounded especially appealing during a Fairbanks winter), a youth service trip to a camp deep in the interior of Alaska, and a group going to help clear trees and brush at the property of a couple in the congregation about an hour away (anyone who helped out got free firewood).

***

Our flight from Alaska to Hawaii had a twelve-hour layover in Seattle, so once again Grant and Paige met us at the airport. We traded our Alaska bag for our Hawaii bag, spent a short night at a Rodeway Inn and left for Hawaii the next morning.

In one sense, our visits to Alaska and Hawaii were similar. In both, geography (and our shrinking bank account) limited how much of the state we'd be able to see. We limited ourselves to one of Hawaii's many islands for our visit (we certainly didn't have a budget for island hopping or helicopter rides). We knew people on Kauai, and though they couldn't house us, they would help us meet new friends. We chose that island.

Still, we needed a place to sleep and keep our backpacks, and the minivan back on the East Coast wasn't an option. We researched hotels, but prices were out of our range. We got excited when we heard that beach camping was available in some areas for the amazing price of $3.00 a night, but Hawaii's bureaucratic hidden deadlines and dependence on fax technology (and maybe our lack of attention to small print) defeated us. We'd put out a Facebook request, but friends and family who'd kindly offered to let us use their timeshares quickly learned that the July 4th weekend (when we'd scheduled our visit to Hawaii) was universally unavailable.

Then a friend asked if we'd checked Airbnb. Mindy scoffed privately until she remembered she hadn't looked there yet. I was sure the prices wouldn't be any better than hotels, and we were getting a little desperate. Mindy checked.

A few blocks from the beach in Kapa'a, where we hoped to stay, we discovered a couple who rent out tents in their yard. Along with a waterproof tent, they supply sleeping bags, a flush porta potty, outdoor showers (with plenty of hot water), and an outdoor kitchen with a microwave, coffee maker, grill, camping stove, refrigerator and (unbelievably) power outlets and wifi. Incredibly, all this cost about the same as the cabin where we'd camped in Alabama, and less than most motel rooms anywhere. We were surprised that the homeowners had both Trump posters and pot plants, but there were also coconut palms, a tidal canal, and even a random stray cat. We had nothing to complain about.

There were plenty of times during the year that we wanted to complain, like when I was on my back under the van putting snow chains on, or when I was on my back in the van desperately trying to sleep. Floating on my back in the Pacific, taking in the beauty of the beach and the blue sky and the blue water, though, really was the best experience my back had all year. We didn't even mind all the roosters.

***

Everyone we met at Sam's Ocean View Restaurant and Bar had a uniquely Hawaiian perspective on what a good bar needs. They all seemed to think the best feature a bar can have is "a beautiful ocean view."

We'd seen bars in the contiguous 48 with a tropical theme, which can be fun even when it's a bit tacky. It's much more fun to watch *Blue Hawaii* on the TV, notice island decorations on the wall, and choose among tropical drinks on the menu when you really are in an island paradise and you can look over the balcony onto a palm tree studded beach.

Mindy and I chose tropical drinks because it just seemed right. I had a Mai Tai, and Mindy went with a Two Palms, which had coconut water as an ingredient. When we first got to the Airbnb, our host sliced open a fresh coconut (with a machete!) and offered us a drink. We've heard it has many health benefits, but the flavor didn't win us over. Mindy thought she might like it better chilled, and she did enjoy her drink.

She had also mistakenly sat on the barstool already claimed by someone else, which we discovered when a white-haired man in a polo shirt returned to the bar from the restroom. When he returned, he was gracious about the seat theft. We introduced ourselves to Andreas and in our conversation mentioned our bar blog. He said he might get around seeing the blog come Tuesday when he got to the library. He doesn't have a computer or a smartphone ("I'm a -- what do you call it? -- a Luddite.") He introduced us to his friend, Laura, who, like Andreas, was originally from the mainland but has lived in Hawaii for years. Laura said she'd always wanted to live on a tropical island.

We asked her what she looked for in a bar, and she told us she appreciated a good wine selection, but that's a challenge on Kauai. "Ninety percent of everything is shipped first to Oahu and then to Kauai which greatly increases the cost." Thankfully, the other thing she looks for is more available. "I want to be treated special," she said.

I also talked to Sam, the bar's owner and manager. She mentioned that July would mark the one year anniversary of when she got the keys to the property, but that the restaurant and bar had opened in October. She'd worked and hung out in restaurants and bars for years, but this was her first management/ownership experience.

She said a good bar needed three things: a bartender who's friendly and competent ("A bartender has to be willing to go outside what they think a drink should be to make what a customer wants"); quality ingredients; and atmosphere (by which she meant lighting, music, and people). Sam admitted that some of the factors that make a good restaurant are a special challenge on Kauai. Fresh ingredients are sometimes hard to come by. One morning she was didn't have enough eggs for the breakfast menu, and didn't have any local sources to get more. "How can you do breakfast without eggs?"

As Laura had noticed regarding wine selection on the island, getting supplies for the bar can be a challenge as well. Sam said she is adjusting and learning to plan well ahead and buy up when things are available.

She also mentioned the challenge of hiring good staff, because people live on the islands for same reason people vacation on the islands. The laid-back lifestyle can conflict with the work ethic that helps a bar run well. Sam seemed invigorated by meeting the challenges of the area -- and by the unique advantage of her bar's beach view.

Sam said she wasn't much of a churchgoer. In fact, she'd consider herself an agnostic or atheist, but even so, she said a church should be "100 percent about acceptance, living the model of love. That's the huge element that is missing; it should be all about tolerance." She recommended the Church of the Pacific because of the wonderful musical events they hosted. She said the church had a good reputation "even with people who aren't into church."

***

Though we eventually did ride the bus past the Church of the Pacific, we already had a different church to visit. We had a connection, a somewhat distant connection, with Kauai Christian Fellowship. One of my nieces is good friends with the daughter of one of the pastors of the church -- and we also knew of the church because of the movie *Soul Surfer*.

Bethany Hamilton was a thirteen-year-old surfer who lost her arm in a shark attack in 2003. The story of that attack and her recovery from it was told first in a best-selling autobiography, then in a feature film released in 2011, both entitled *Soul Surfer*. Her family attended Kauai Christian Fellowship.

The church sometimes got *Soul Surfer* tourists who were disappointed because they expect the real-life church to be exactly like the one in the film. The church met temporarily in a tent in the parking lot, the film placed the tent on the edge of the beach. Since then, the church has moved into a building on the property.

Back in the day, the church (founded by Pastor Steve Thompson, the father of our niece's friend) was called North Shore Christian Fellowship, but recently the congregation merged with Kauai Christian Fellowship. The two congregations meet on different campuses but gather together for events and share the pastoral staff.

Before the service, a ukulele choir played several songs, including "How Great Thou Art" in Hawaiian and English. We sat in the front row on the comfy chairs and couches, not at the round tables on the sides with snacks and beverages. (Both are designed to keep people from hiding and huddling in the back rows.)

During the greeting time, I shook hands with actor Craig T. Nelson, a member of the church and friend of Bethany Hamilton (the surfer) and her family, who had asked that Nelson play the doctor in *Soul Surfer*. I was excited to meet the voice of Bob Parr, "Mr. Incredible" from the Pixar classic, *The Incredibles*.

We'd heard there'd be snacks after worship, but the long table in the back of the gymnasium held enough food for a meal. There were cookies, a frosted cake, more cookies, pastries and jam, pasta salad, mandarin oranges, devilled eggs, and Peeps. People apologized for what they said was a smaller selection than usual, maybe because the church Fourth of July picnic was the next day. Another explanation we heard was that it was a good surf day, and those who brought food figured not many would stick around after church.

As I talked to people during lunch, I asked what they appreciated about the church. I noticed the word "family" came up about as frequently as "community." Mason Bundschuh, the worship pastor, said that family focus wasn't just a part of the church but also part of the island culture. We saw children riding skateboards on the concrete floor of the worship area, but there were always plenty of "aunties" and "uncles" keeping a watchful eye.

The church fostered a sense of family, and formality wasn't particularly valued. Rick Bundschuh, one of the church's teaching pastors and (according to the church website) resident troublemaker, told me about their membership process. They invite everyone who wants to be part of the church to a big party, a barbeque, where they discuss the church, its goals, and how they go about meeting those goals. If people want to become a part of the church, they reach into a bowl for their own key to the church (the South Campus, not the North Campus school building. That wouldn't make any sense). Hundreds of people have the keys to that church property. "If we err, we'd prefer to err on the side of trust," Rick said.

If you were wondering whether Soul Surfer, Bethany Hamilton herself, was at the church that morning: she was not. We heard that she still attends on occasion, but she's now married and a mother, with other commitments (including the Bethany Hamilton Foundation), and she mostly lives on the mainland. For a while, we heard, tourists were coming to church to look at her, so she and her family had to arrive late and leave early to avoid distracting other worshipers. Kahu (Pastor) Steve Thompson told us about a ministry Bethany had started ("Beautifully Flawed") for other women who had also lost limbs, and he mentioned that she has also been able to bring families to Hawaii through the Make-a-Wish Foundation. She has become a public face for the good work the church has been doing for years.

Riding with Kahu Thompson to the church's Fourth of July picnic on Monday was one of the two times we rode in a car on the island (on Saturday, longtime friends drove us to some of the most beautiful sites on the north and east side of Kauai). The picnic was at a beach several miles off the bus route, so Kahu Thompson picked us up in time to help set up for the event. . Even with cool, windy rain and no fireworks at all, celebrating Independence Day in the 50th US state was amazing.

On Tuesday morning, we loaded up our backpacks and took a bus to the airport (with a stop at a nearby movie theater to see *Central Intelligence*, a silly caper set mostly in Maryland). We caught a red-eye flight to Seattle.

We caught another bus to Paige and Grant's apartment, and we were looking forward to spending a week with them and with our son Bret (who'd flown in from Santa Rosa, California) and daughter Jil (who we'd seen only a few weeks before in New York). We appreciated the time with them and enjoyed the odd (for us, anyway) opportunity to have our usual state experiences (bar, church, movie) with them.

By the time we flew back to JFK, Mindy was a little homesick -- for the van. During the three weeks we'd been away from it, she'd continually realized some random thing she wanted -- maybe the cheese grater or a sweater -- was in the van at her college roommate's house on the East Coast. After a great time with our kids, we were ready to be reunited with our little metal home on wheels.

***

We took the train from JFK to Darien, Connecticut (state #29!). Our friend Carrie picked us up for a few days at her house.

The next morning, we started the van and heard a sound worse than the crack that announced the death of our laptop. As we headed down Carrie's driveway, the van started shaking and making ominous rattling sounds. I pulled over (panicking a bit), and Mindy texted Carrie at work to see if she'd noticed anything while we were gone.

Carrie had started the van up and moved it a few times while we were gone, but everything had seemed fine. I started the engine again, and the rattling and shaking seemed a little worse than before. Mindy asked Carrie what mechanic she recommended; we were able to get an appointment for the next morning.

That night I kept thinking about "what ifs." What if the whole engine or the transmission is broken? What if the mechanic says, "Your car is dead?" We'd been able to pay for everything so far, but we didn't have money for significant repairs. We certainly didn't have money for a car, even if we knew enough about cars to buy a used car that wouldn't break down along the way (we definitely didn't). If the minivan could be repaired, what if the repair shop couldn't get parts, or the repairs would take a long time? What if we lost a week, or even two of travel time? Could we still make it to every state in a year?

What if the trip was over?

I took the car, rattling and shaking, to the shop the next day. The guy at the shop told me it needed new spark plugs. Just spark plugs. The bill was about $400; we could afford that, especially if we camped and stayed with friends (or slept in the minivan) for the next month instead of spending money at motels.

I drove back to Carrie's, we loaded the stuff we'd stored at her house while we were gone, and we were back on the road.

9
SUMMERING

 With so many states jammed together in such a small area, we were frequently shocked to realize that Rhode Island (or, for that matter, Vermont) had two Senators, just like California. In the West, you can drive all day without leaving the state, but in New England, it's easy to drive through several states in a few hours. We spent most of July and all of August in those states, got to know a lot of people, and put plenty of miles on the minivan...still, all those stories fit into this one chapter.

***

We'd already heard many times that people went to church or a bar for the sense of community they found there. Moviegoing, on the other hand, was easy to think of as a solitary experience. Theaters tend to be dark; ideally, people don't talk to each other, and yet, we met people who appreciated the community aspect of film viewing.

I'd been part of an online community for movie lovers, Hollywood Elsewhere, for several years. Before the trip began, I posted there that we hoped to go to the movies in every state. Some people at the site suggested meeting up along the road, but nothing came of it until we got to Massachusetts. Paul, who I'd known only as his Hollywood Elsewhere avatar, suggested meeting at Jordan's Furniture in Reading. We were a little confused.

It turns out, Jordan's Furniture is more than a furniture store. It's also the location of an IMAX theater. Fenway's Green Monster was also in residence; there's a ropes course, a display of "Beantown" made from jelly beans, an ice cream shop, and a fountain with a light and music show (This wasn't a place that valued subtlety). Jordan's also had a Fuddruckers, where Paul said we should meet.

Over very large burgers, I asked Paul about his favorite movie-going experiences. He talked about watching movies with his parents and with his daughter. He told about seeing *Pulp Fiction* with friends and getting together with friends for *Star Wars* debuts. He's a real movie fan, but every memory was more about the people he went with than about the movies they saw. The movie we saw together, *Star Trek Beyond,* was quite forgettable, but getting to know Paul in person was something to remember.

***

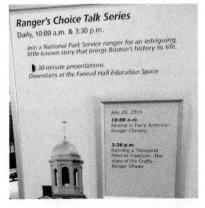

We stayed with Mindy's childhood friend, Jayne, who lived in a Boston suburb but commuted to work in the city. She escorted us onto the train and off it, showed us her office near the Boston Common, and walked us to the start of the Freedom Trail.

The Freedom Trail, a red brick, two and a half mile walk, touched sixteen historically significant sites from the Revolutionary War and other aspects of eighteenth-century American history. As we walked, we were struck by how much of that history was connected to churches and bars.

Among our stops was Faneuil Hall, where many great and important speeches were made in the public meeting rooms -- and alcohol was served in the market area. We met Chelsey, a ranger with the National Park Service, who on that particular day (and at the time we happened to be on the site) was giving a talk about alcohol's role in colonial days. Was the timing serendipity or God's intervention?

Taverns, she told us, were a vital part of colonial life, often serving as post offices and courthouses. With the full approval of the community, they were an important part of daily life, often located next to schools and churches. Chelsey said her research indicated that people drank more back in that day, averaging nine gallons of hard liquor per person a year (as opposed to the contemporary American average of three gallons).

Some of the founding fathers were brewers, but we heard that Samuel Adams wasn't very good at it and that the brewery with his name was founded after he was gone. Though the facts have been lost over the years, it was rumored that the Boston Tea Party was planned at the Green Dragon Tavern a block or two from Faneuil Hall.

Several churches along the Freedom Walk caught our attention, including Park Street Church (an abolitionist stronghold half a century after the American Revolution), King's Chapel (which understandably stood vacant during the Revolutionary War years), Old South Meeting House (a Congregational Church that was also used as a planning site for revolutionaries), and, of course, Old North Church (of "One if by land" fame in Paul Revere's warning ride). Aside from the Old South Meeting House, most of the churches are still active. We thought about our friend Jessica from Washington D.C. as we looked around Old North; she'd mentioned it was her home church.

Mindy and I should have been caught up in the amazing way our trip themes were blending with American history as we walked that 2 ½ mile path. But the day was really warm (for Boston), in the upper 90's, and we hadn't remembered to bring water bottles. We were hot and cranky and sniping at each other.

Typically, when conversation lags, it's common for one of us to say to the other, "You're wonderful." Usually, the other person responds in kind, and it's nice. But when I said this to Mindy as we walked up a steep incline on the Freedom Trail -- probably Beacon Hill or something else historically significant that we didn't appreciate much at the moment, she said, "Just stop talking." So I did. Did I mention it was quite warm and we were really thirsty?

Almost as big a vexation for Mindy as the heat was her phone. She had forgotten to charge it before we left, and we'd been using it to find our way around. She was afraid the battery would die before we got back to where we were meeting Jayne. I've learned that when Mindy's phone is troubled, she is troubled.

Later, when we were willing to talk to each other again, we agreed we'd probably enjoy the pictures and memories of the walk more than we enjoyed the walk itself.

***

Near the end of the trail was a different Boston landmark, a touchstone for our trip.

A surprising number of people told us that a good bar was "You know, like *Cheers*, where everybody knows your name." That TV show premiered before Mindy and I met, but we heard that response not just from geezers like ourselves, but also from millennials. We thought the answer was kind of funny since on the show the characters are often rotten to each other, but people remember the theme song.

While the show was on the air, the bar across the street from Boston Public Gardens was known as "The Bull and Finch," but that's no longer true. Possibly for the benefit of tourism, the bar that provided the exterior for *Cheers* location shooting was renamed "Cheers," and they rebuilt a section of the interior to look like the bar in the show. When we arrived in the early afternoon, we didn't see any seats at the bar in the original downstairs location or in the upstairs replica. We were grouchy enough at the time that we didn't feel like talking to folks anyway, even to ask our usual bar questions. We were okay with skipping a drink then anyway since the place seemed a lot more like a tourist attraction than a real bar.

Still, after we'd gotten water at the drinking fountain, I was glad to get a selfie with a Norm standup cutout. After a few more minutes of looking at the crowds at the iconic bar, we decided we'd rather spend the rest of the afternoon in the cool solitude of the Boston Public Library.

***

When I was young, my Aunt Lola gave me a knock-knock joke book that I loved. I don't think she expected me to use it to get into a bar in Manchester, New Hampshire.

There was no sign for the place on the street. Even though we knew the address, we weren't quite confident that the business listed as "8ne5" was what we were looking for. We headed up the narrow stairway. At the top, we read, "Looking for a password?" on a signboard near an old-fashioned phone booth.

Mindy had already looked up the password on Facebook (it's also available if you follow the bar on Twitter or Instagram), so she went in the phone booth first. After she said the password, she jumped when the brick wall next to the phone booth slid aside, and a hostess welcomed her in.

I wanted to do something different, so when I had the chance to give the password, I said I didn't know it. The voice in the phonebooth asked for a knock-knock joke. I'd carefully considered which joke from the book I should use -- "Robin" "Robin who?" "I'm robbin' you, so hand over all your money!" might suggest criminal intent, so I didn't do that one. "Denial" "Denial who?" "De Nile is a river in Egypt" might be too cerebral for the occasion.

Eventually, I went with, "Knock Knock," "Who's there?" "Artichoke," "Artichoke who?" "Artie chokes when he eats too fast."

It did the trick. The hostess opened the brick wall, and I was in.

As the wall closed behind me, I looked around. The decor was a mix of prohibition era styling with splashes of modern art. One back wall had the staff's mugshots along with information about various drinks. I got a traditional drink called Vieux Carre in honor of our friends at Vieux Carre Baptist in New Orleans, and we talked with Meg, the bartender. She told us that 815 doesn't buy advertising, instead relying on social media and word of mouth to bring in a steady stream of visitors and regulars.

The speakeasy doesn't just use social media to their own advantage; they shared our post about our visit, and our page views went way up. We started to think that churches should learn something about publicity from bars.

***

"And we put the couch in the showers," Elliot added, after listing all the other things (like office equipment, a canoe, and everything from various girls' tents) that he and his brother had moved into the showers at camp.

"That was my grandfather's couch!" Chip exclaimed in mock horror.

We were visiting Chip and Cathy, whose daughter was one of our daughter Jil's roommates. (Connections became convoluted on the trip.) Years ago, Cathy had run a summer camp in New Hampshire. Elliot, one of their former campers and another friend of their daughter's, was staying with them the same night we were. As happens with people who were at camp together, the memories and stories flowed, along with the usual amazement that more injuries didn't occur during those wild adventures in the woods. Anyone who went to summer camp as a kid (or watched *Meatballs* or *Friday the 13th*) knows camp has a knack for building lifelong memories.

For example: when I was in elementary school, I had a nightmare about heaven. Chilly Willy, the cartoon penguin, drowned in the ocean, and then he was sitting on a cloud and strumming a harp. It all looked so boring! That summer at Calvin Crest, a Presbyterian camp just outside of Yosemite, the speaker said, "Jesus said, 'I came to give you life and abundant life.' You know all the games, swimming, hiking, and the great beauty of the mountains you've experienced this week? These are all gifts from God, and He has even better things waiting for us in heaven!" That took care of my fear of a boring afterlife, and when they invited us to walk through a door frame (because Jesus called Himself the door) as a symbol of entering life in Christ. I walked through the door.

So we thought we'd try to visit a church camp. Before Mindy was born, her dad had attended a conference at Pilgrim Pines camp in New Hampshire. We googled it and found out that they host a series of family camps throughout the summer on the shores of Lake Swanzey. Along with cabins and a retreat center, the camp has a campground where we could pitch our tent for a few days while attending some of the gatherings of the family camp.

We arrived at an odd time: Friday afternoon on the last full day of that particular Family Camp (Week 5). We attended the talent show that served as a culmination of the week's activities. Groups of friends, individuals, and large families all had their moments in the spotlight. Musical numbers by children and teens ranged from adorable to excellent. A kid named Owen demonstrated his prowess with the Rubik's Cube. There were classic camp skits such as the Banana/Bandana "Magic" Act (it gets messy). Then there were presentations from the classes of kids that met together throughout the week. The high schoolers' parody of ABBA's "Dancing Queen" was the highlight.

The next morning, many campers said their goodbyes, took final photos, and exchanged social media connections. A few hours later, we saw the new families arrive, with all the excitement of people seeing the beauty of the lake for the first time or delighting in a return. In a way, our experience was a taste of what the summer staff got to experience; they see people come and go from the beginning of July through the middle of August.

We were able to enjoy some of the camp activities: kayaking, swimming, family crafts, and family games. Even better, we were able to worship with fellow campers. We've talked to many people who say, "I don't go to church; I worship God in nature." It was good to be at a church camp where we could enjoy both.

***

Our understanding of clergy in the Unitarian Universalist Association was that in general, a belief in God (let alone a belief in Jesus as the Son of God) wasn't a requirement. So we'd decided we wouldn't go to Unitarian Universalist Churches -- but we did end up going to hear a Unitarian Universalist chaplain preach.

I frequent the political website, *Ricochet*, and that's where I came in contact with a Maine Game Warden Service chaplain named Kate Braestrup. I asked if we could meet her in a bar, and she asked if we'd come to hear her preach.

We first got together with her at the Drouthy Bear Pub in Camden, Maine. Since we were in a bar, we asked our two questions, "What makes for a good bar?" and "What makes for a good church?"

She said that a good bar was "someplace within walking distance of my house," adding that she'd like to be able to walk to get a coffee in the morning and walk to get a beer in the evening. Andrew Stewart, the owner of the pub we were enjoying, was considering building such a place near Kate's home.

As for what makes for a good church, Kate said, "At the moment, political diversity; ideological diversity." She argued that our inability to listen to people with different opinions is going to "make us stupid." She also appreciated good music and an enthusiastic choir. She said she likes small churches because, "I like knowing people; knowing and being known." She laughingly added, "I appreciate a thought-provoking, brilliant sermon," especially when she's preaching.

I found it interesting that Kate talked about the need for ideological diversity in a congregation. Many people we spoke to in bars mentioned the need for racial diversity and the need to be "accepting," which usually seemed to mean "accepting of the LGBTQ community." Kate's concern was more about acceptance of a different group: officials in law enforcement. Her concern made sense, since Maine Game Wardens are law enforcement officers, and Kate's the widow of a Maine Highway Patrol officer who died in the line of duty.

I asked her how churches can make police officers welcome.

"First of all," she answered, "Don't have a giant Black Lives Matter banner hanging in front of your church." since that tends to translate as "we welcome people who think about this issue the way we do." Since many in the BLM movement tend to consider those in law enforcement racist, such a banner might dissuade a police officer from coming to that church.

I asked Kate what other things might keep a police officer from coming to church. She said that some churches, especially more liberal congregations "make a big deal about bringing a gun into church." Churches sometimes designate themselves no gun zones. For a police officer, the gun is part of the uniform. If a church says, "You can't bring a gun in church," it's saying to a uniformed police officer, "You can't come to church."

She went on to say that churches should be educated on the role of law enforcement in society. "Especially in theologically liberal denominations, police are misunderstood." She finds this most unfortunate because, "It's good for a church to have police officers around, and good for police officers to go to church."

I asked the obvious follow-up question: "How do churches benefit from having police officers in the congregation?"

"Police officers are natural theologians," Kate said. "They have to deal with practical issues of theology in their day to day experience, such as why bad things happen to good people and the problem of evil." They aren't dealing with abstractions, but reality. She mentioned her daughter's work combating child pornography, a very concrete manifestation of evil, and suggested pastors should go on ride alongs with police officers to get a different perspective on the community they both serve.

I asked how police officers benefit from church. She said that police officers "deal with people at their worst on a day to day basis. At best, they're dealing with people having a really bad day. It's good for them to be around people at their best." Police officers might even be encouraged by the announcements in a church -- they see so many problems in a community that they can't address, but hearing that people are feeding the hungry or providing activities for neighborhood kids can be encouraging. Officers can find it helpful to realize that other people are sharing the burden of caring for the community.

Anyway, we went to hear Kate preach at Hancock Chapel. The Chapel was celebrating their 119th summer of bringing speakers to the summer resort community. In the course of the summer, residents and guests would hear from other Unitarian Universalists, Episcopalians, a rabbi, and a Buddhist.

Kate's sermon was on fear. She noted that people tend to be frightened of young men. This isn't a phenomenon of one culture; studies show that people throughout the world are more afraid of young men than any other group of people. "Isn't it interesting," she asked, "that when God decided to show Himself to the world, He did so in as a young man?" She went on to encourage the congregation to learn to "Fear Not" by trusting God rather than our past experiences.

I loved Kate's sermon and sent her an email to tell her so, and I included a bit of teasing. "You know, Kate, for a Unitarian, you sure talk about Jesus a lot."

She responded, "That's because I'm a Christian. I don't think being a Unitarian and a Christian are mutually exclusive things. Though there are people in my denomination who don't agree about that."

***

We'd hoped to spend our first night in Vermont at a combination drive-in movie theater/motel, which sounded like a cool thing. We'd read you could rent a room and watch the drive-in movie through your motel window. When we arrived, we found the place looked shabby, and the rooms -- even from the outside -- looked a little frightening. We thought of just going to the movie, but it was the latest DC superhero film ("Make mine Marvel!"), and I'd been actively trying to avoid *Suicide Squad*. The admission price wasn't cheap, but then we found out there was a surcharge if you brought food in -- and we always had food with us. That's part of life on the road.

So we drove on, looking for a cheap (not scary) motel or a campground. We certainly didn't think we could afford anything as nice as the Stratford Inn (from *Newhart*, our Vermont-set TV show). Eventually, we found a dark parking space beside a laundromat and fell asleep in the minivan. We were up at 5:00 am (we figured laundromats probably opened pretty early) and located a McDonald's for the free wi-fi. We realized that Montpelier, the state capital was only about fifteen minutes away.

When we got there, we were happy to find a library and a decent motel. We spent the morning writing posts at the library, checked into the motel on the other side of the tracks, and as the rain started drizzling down, headed to our bar for the week, World Famous Charlie-O's.

The sign above the door boasted "Good Drinks and Bad Company since the War Between the States." The previous weekend the bar had celebrated their 40th anniversary. You don't have to be a math whiz or history buff to notice a discrepancy. We asked Beckie, the bartender and an assistant manager, to help us wrestle with those concepts. She said the building had been a bar since the Civil War, but the bar had only been called Charlie-O's for the past 40 years.

***

We left Montpelier on Tuesday, but we still needed to find a church and a community to focus on. Since we could go anywhere, we decided on the town of Waterbury. It's the home of Ben and Jerry's Ice Cream, and the factory tour was a bargain, $3 a person, so we took the tour and enjoyed the free samples at the end. Afterward, we looked around the cemetery for dead flavors (Holy Cannoli, Wavy Gravy, Peanuts! Popcorn!, Schweddy Balls, and many more).

We found a campground where we could stay that Wednesday night, but all they were sold out for Thursday, Friday, and Saturday. We'd need to sleep someplace else for the weekend. Still, we decided to visit the Wednesday night prayer meeting at Living Hope Wesleyan.

There are church services where a visitor can blend into the background and not be noticed. Your average Wednesday night prayer meeting is not such a service. There was a nice little group, but we were quite obviously strangers, and we appreciated being warmly welcomed. People asked about us, and we were more than happy to talk about our trip. Eventually, people asked where we were staying.

Before we went to New England, we'd been warned that the region might not be friendly; people kept to themselves. But after mentioning we needed a place to stay, one person offered space to pitch our tent in their yard. Another person offered the trailer parked in their driveway. And Dennis, who was the first person to respond, offered us a bed in his house. Three people offered to let us stay with them, though they'd known us for less than an hour.

Part of the reason for this trip was to see if God's Church was still alive and working in America. These simple acts of hospitality reminded us that indeed it is.

10

FOUR SERMONS

Mindy and I started the trip with a little over $30,000 in the bank and the expectation of about $6,000 more coming in during the year from our tax refund, royalties on my *Bill the Warthog* kids' mysteries, and my mom's estate. We knew it would be difficult to make those funds last the whole year, so we stretched our money as far as we could. We enjoyed the hospitality of friends, family and even, to our eternal gratitude, strangers. We stayed in the least expensive motels we could find (and collected points so we could enjoy the occasional free night), camped, and, of course, slept in the van.

Denny's was too rich for our blood. Wendy's, on the other, had a 4 for $4 special. A burger, fries, chicken nuggets and a refillable drink made for an excellent dinner for the two of us. In motels, sometimes the jelly from the "continental breakfast" supplied our lunch as well (we generally had peanut butter and crackers tucked somewhere in our food box).

Still, there were larger, unavoidable expenses. Visiting all fifty states meant flights to Alaska and Hawaii, and though we managed happily with the bus system in Hawaii, in Alaska, we needed a rental car. Oil changes and the car repair in Connecticut were reasonable expenses.

By mid-August, we had months and miles to go, but our bank account had sunk to the low side of four digits. Until then, we'd been paying off the airplane-miles-accumulating credit card every month, but we realized that for the rest of the year, we'd only be able to make minimum payments.

At the beginning of the year, we hadn't expected that the generosity of friends and family would provide $110 per month. We'd sold one article for about $200, and we expected another check or two from my mom's estate. That was the income we could expect for the rest of the year.

I was worried. What would happen if we completely ran out of money? Would we have to stop in Mayfield and get jobs as crossing guards and fast food workers?.

***

This is probably a good time to mention how amazed we were throughout the trip by people's willingness to open their homes to strangers. We'd mentioned to missionary friends that we hadn't been to a Brethren church and that we didn't have a destination in mind for New Jersey. They got in touch with other missionaries who let us know about three different churches that might be interesting, and they suggested people to contact at those churches.

A few weeks later, we rang the doorbell at Allan and Fiona's house in northern New Jersey. They opened the door a crack and asked us for ID, then laughed and welcomed us like we were family. After we'd been in their home for a couple of days, I asked Allan why they took us -- complete strangers -- into their home and their lives.

He explained that a few years earlier, he'd decided to walk to Toronto, where he and Fiona had grown up and where their sons live now. The trek took about three weeks, and along the way, people had greeted him and offered a glass of water, a meal, or even a bed for the night. After the trip, Allan told Fiona that from that time forward whenever anyone asked to stay with them, if it were at all possible, the guest would be welcome.

Allan said another reason they took people in came from Scripture, Hebrews 13:2 "Do not forget to show hospitality to strangers, for by doing so people have shown hospitality to angels without knowing it." (In this we certainly disappointed them.)

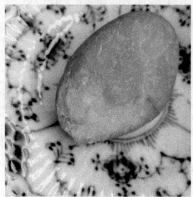 Fiona and Allan took us for a walk along the Jersey Shore, where Mindy was surprised to find what looked like a fresh roll on the sand. For some reason, it looked like the seagulls had taken a bite but left the rest of the bread alone, so she reached down to pick it up.

To her surprise, the "roll" was a rock. She laughed about getting a rock when she expected bread, and she slipped it into her purse as a reminder of God's provision.

***

Hospitality in New Jersey was the first time we relied on friends of friends to find a destination, but it wouldn't be the last. Even though Mindy been born in Cincinnati, Ohio, and had spent her elementary school years in East Cleveland, we hadn't found any friends we could stay with. As we'd done a couple of times before, we asked our Facebook friends if anyone knew anyone in Ohio, and John, who I knew from my childhood church, had a Facebook friend, David, in

Ohio. John and David had never actually met, but John had known David's father and…well, the short version is that David said we could stay with his family outside Toledo.

But we had an important stop to make before we could visit them and learn about their ministry. We needed to find out what was happening at the East Cleveland church Mindy's dad had served from 1966 through 1972.

The church is still there, but it hasn't been Historic First Presbyterian for years. The big stone building has had a lot of names since Mindy's family moved away, and now it's the New Life Cathedral, an independent congregation. During the late 1960s, the neighborhood had been home to an ethnically diverse group of families whose kids played together in the street, the vacant lot, the ravine, and the church graveyard. The members of the church, though, had mostly moved to nearby suburbs, and most of them were white. These days, the church and the neighborhood seem to be almost exclusively African American.

The old house where Mindy grew up had long ago been torn down to make room for parking. Mindy paced the parking spaces, telling me where each room had been. One of the church doors was open, so we went inside. The room Mindy remembered as the church parlor was alive with activity. It was a Tuesday, and some older women were sitting at a table on one side of the room. A younger woman approached us, asking if we were picking anyone up (the activities for senior citizens were finishing up for the day). We explained why we were there, and she said we could look around, but that another woman, Angela, had the key to the sanctuary.

We looked around the basement, where Mindy recalled a lot of church dinners and a party the night before she broke out in chicken pox. As far as she could tell, the inside of the church had improved over the years. We went back upstairs to the entryway by the church office, where we met Angela.

She let us into the sanctuary by the same door Mindy remembered. The sanctuary, with grey stone walls, stained glass windows, and dark wood pews, looked exactly the way Mindy remembered it. After we took a few photos, Mindy asked where Angela had grown up.

Two sentences later, they realized they'd had the same first-grade teacher, Mrs. Bibb, and they'd been in the same class. Both had loved their teacher, and Angela told Mindy that Mrs. Bibb had gone on to teach at the college level, where Angela had been her student again.

After a quick hug and a promise to pray, we said goodbye to Angela and East Cleveland. We had to be at a worship service in Toledo that night, where we would meet David, our friend's Facebook friend, and his wife, Kelly.

***

We knew they worked with a ministry to the poor in South Toledo, but we didn't know what to expect. The worship service (and dinner after, both part of Mosaic Ministries) was held in a building that was obviously an old school. It still is, of a kind: it's the home of Baby University.

Kelly is a slender blonde woman who has a calm competence that I'm sure serves her well as director of Baby U. She showed us a room lined with short bookshelves filled with children's books; more children's books were stacked on tables.

Unlike most universities, Baby U doesn't sell these textbooks at exorbitant prices. All the books are given away to parents along with diapers, formula, and clothes. The goal with all of the freebies is encouraging new or expectant parents to attend Baby U classes where they could learn life skills, child-rearing strategies, nutrition information, and other important parenting help.

Mosaic ministers to a community where good parenting is rarely modeled. Kelly told us about another ministry, the Beauty Project, which aims to teach middle school-aged girls that they were more than their outward appearance. Kelly sometimes brought the girls to her house to make cookies or other treats, and one day, one of the girls remarked how unusual Kelly and David were. Kelly asked why, and the girl answered that they were the only people she knew who were married and had jobs.

David told about helping a man get a job. He'd also performed a marriage ceremony for the man and his girlfriend. A few weeks after the wedding, the woman told David, "My husband has abandoned me."

That didn't sound like the man David knew, so he asked the woman to explain. "Every day, he leaves me alone all day," she said.

"Isn't he going to his job?" David asked.

"He abandons me," she insisted. He was going to work, and she didn't like being left alone. People going to work every day wasn't normal in her world, it meant she'd been abandoned.

Being around this kind of poverty made me look at our shrinking bank account differently. We had always been able to assume that even if we went broke, even if we couldn't complete the mission we'd set for ourselves, we could go to work somewhere and rebuild. David and Kelly were serving people who had no idea how to change the lives they were leading and no tools to make any changes.

Along with their team, David and Kelly pursued the goal of changing lives for the better through a "Transformation Pipeline" that included

Baby University, a partnership with Toledo Day School, a program to help adults get their GEDs, and a finance class. Their primary mission, though, was the spiritual transformation of individuals and the community through the Gospel of Jesus Christ.

***

Throughout the trip we'd tell people we were going to "a church and bar" in every state, and time and again people would ask "A church in a bar?" Sometimes they misheard, usually, they were joking, but David and Kelly did take us to a church in a bar (or a bar in a church, depending on how you looked at it).

The Black Cloister Pub was definitely in an interesting neighborhood of downtown Toledo. The Toledo Mud Hens stadium was just a couple of blocks away, and we were able to wander into the stadium to watch a few minutes of the last inning or two. Also within easy walking distance: a strip club that had help wanted signs advertising college scholarship programs for dancers.

The brewpub is decorated in an early German Reformation style, including a portrait of Martin Luther on the wall "autographed" by Martin himself, sending his good wishes to the pub. The "95 Heroes" who contributed to a Kickstarter campaign to open the brewhouse are listed on the wall in a nod to Luther's 95 Theses.

We were there on a Friday night; the servers were cheerful, and the atmosphere was friendly. Our waitress spoke highly Tom Schaeffer, her boss and the founder, CEO, President, and head of marketing (and long-time brewer) of the Black Cloister. He's also the pastor of Threshold Lutheran Church.

We went back on Sunday morning to see what the bar looked like as a church. That morning a photographer from *Living Lutheran* magazine was taking pictures of the unique ministry for an upcoming article. Tom Schaeffer greeted us, and I asked how the dual project got started.

He said the church had come first -- when they got started about ten years ago, they met in a different bar, then in schools and homes, but hadn't been able to find a permanent place. Since people in the congregation knew of his love for brewing and beer, they encouraged him to open the brewpub -- which would also be the church's meeting space.

We sat at the bar for the worship service. Tom's sermon was the third in a series on the Lord's Prayer -- this one was on the bit about "give us this day our daily bread." He brought in the "brutal, crazy story" of God's provision of a ram when Abraham was asked sacrifice of his son, Isaac. The essential point of the sermon, which that story reinforced, was that being in a relationship with God means you know He will provide. Since we'd been fretting over how long our money would hold out, that sermon from Matthew 6 was precisely what we needed to hear.

As the service closed with the final hymn, a bartender was setting up to serve.

Late that afternoon, we went back to South Toledo for Mosaic's Sunday service. David had a guest speaker, a Baptist, who spoke on the Lord's Prayer and about God's provision. Mindy and I turned to each other, and one of us whispered, "Okay, God, we get it."

***

We left Ohio to spend the next week in Michigan with my nephew who lived in Wolverine Lake, a suburb of Detroit. Jonathan's kids live in

Minnesota during the school year, so we were able to use their Lego packed, *Star Wars* decorated room.

It was good to have time with Jonathan, but we wanted to see Detroit. With its variety of upheavals over the past few years, the city itself is fascinating, but we were most interested in the great number of refugees from the Middle East that come to the city and the surrounding suburbs.

Our first visit to the Arab-American Friendship Center proved awkward, since we'd inadvertently come during women-only classes. We arranged to meet Dwight Billingsley, the center's director, during registration for co-ed English and citizenship classes the next evening.

The Center is justifiably proud that graduates of their program have a near perfect record passing citizenship exams. Dwight told us many interesting stories about interactions with their Arab students, but one, in particular, struck us.

During an English language class a few years ago, a number of the adult Arab students were discussing their plans for the upcoming holiday of Eid al-Adha. Dwight was teaching the class and asked what students knew about the holiday. They responded it was a time of feasting, families gathering, and dressing up. (Much as if you asked many Americans what the Fourth of July was about, they'd respond picnics and fireworks.) Dwight pressed to learn the true significance of the day.

Few of them knew, so Dwight told them the story of God's request that Abraham sacrifice his son, and God's provision of a ram to take the son's place. One of the students asked how he knew so much of their religion. Dwight replied the story predated Muhammad and was in the Biblical book of Genesis. (In Genesis, however, the son was Isaac. Muslim tradition assumed the son was Ishmael.) During the rest of the course, Dwight said, there was as much discussion of religion as there was of language.

We appreciated Dwight's anecdote. It spoke to the Center's goal of providing for immigrants' educational needs, and engaging people in conversation about the Gospel of Jesus Christ -- but it meant something else to us. It brought up the story we'd heard the previous Sunday morning about Abraham and reminded us -- once more -- of God's provision.

***

Mindy and I took pictures of the exterior of the Arabic Evangelical Alliance Church (because we were always taking pictures) but a woman came over and asked what we were doing. I could understand her concern. Since 9/11, Arab Americans have dealt with being suspected of terrorism. For all the woman knew, we planned to accuse the church of being affiliated with ISIS.

While doing a little Wikipedia research, I found an interesting fact: though the majority of Arabs in the world are Muslim, the majority of Arab immigrants to the United States have been Christian (63% according to the Arab American Institute). But since the majority of Arab immigrants to the Detroit area have been Muslims, reporters might carelessly write things that would lead to further Christian/Muslim tension in the Arab community.

Mindy wasn't surprised to learn the woman's husband was the church's senior pastor, the Rev. Dr. Jacob Kakish. We'd noticed that pastor's wives were often a church's best greeter, as well as the most ardent protector.

"Do you know Arabic?" she asked. We admitted we didn't, but we assured her that we'd be fine. We'd been to plenty of worship services in other languages, untranslated. We were looking forward to an Arabic worship service.

Dr. Kakish told us about their unique ministry. Arab Evangelical Alliance Church was one of the few Christian Arab congregations in the States that owned their building. Dr. Kakish came to the area in 1978, and for a time the congregation shared the building with the English language Christian and Missionary Alliance congregation which owned the building. But with demographic shifts in Madison Heights (a Detroit suburb), the English language congregation died out, and the CMA denomination gave the building to the Arab congregation. (Every other Arabic congregation in the area, as far as we could learn, shared their building with an English language congregation and worked around their schedule.)

As the worship service began, Pastor Walid Gammouh brought headphones for Mindy and me, and he translated the songs and the prayers and, of course, the message. A layman, a member of the church, was preaching that evening. He'd chosen Matthew 6:25-34 as his text. This passage, like the Lord's Prayer, is part of Jesus' Sermon on the Mount, as is the Lord's Prayer. The reading began with these words, "Don't worry about your life, what you will eat or drink" and continued with assurances that God as a good Father would provide all that we needed.

As Mindy and I drove back to my nephew's house that night, I said, "So. God seems to be telling us something."

On Sunday morning, as we pulled into the vast parking lot of a suburban megachurch, Mindy said, "If this is another sermon from Matthew 6..."

After a couple of weeks of going to churches that were a bit more gritty, walking into a huge place with white columns and many well washed windows was a change. We were amazed when we saw the stage in the sanctuary.

The summer's worship theme was "Coming Home," the stage contained what looked like an elegant two-story country house. But that wasn't all. There was also a large, realistic oak tree with a tire swing, a big grassy front yard, and a red pick-up truck with cut logs in the back. The thing I found most impressive was the active sprinkler on the "lawn."

I know it isn't fair, but on Friday night I'd talked with Pastor Walid about a ministry he was launching for refugees in Detroit. He mentioned struggles in raising funds for the ministry. Since I serve a Lord who praised a woman for pouring very expensive perfume on His feet, I really shouldn't criticize other people for how they spend their money, but we still wondered how much that set cost.

Nonetheless, if you were wondering about that morning's Bible verses, the sermon -- unlike the previous three we'd heard -- was not from Matthew Chapter 6. It was from Luke Chapter 12, the so-called Sermon on the Plain. The first line of the Scripture reading was verse 22, "Therefore I tell you not to worry about your life, what you will eat..."

Though from a different Gospel, it was basically the same Scripture as Friday night's.

I can't say we stopped worrying about money that day. We continued to see the bank account dribble away, and the credit card balance creep higher, but Mindy and I could at least remind each other, "Was it a coincidence that we heard those four sermons in a row?"

11
ZOMBIES

The accusation could have ruined my life. I was a youth pastor at Central Evangelical Free Church in Minneapolis, nearing three decades ago. A high school senior whose family attended the church was home sick. I decided it was part of my job to encourage her by bringing a care package to her house: fruit, orange juice, and a couple of fashion magazines.

A few days later, Rick, the pastor of the church, knocked on my office door and told me that the church board had received a serious accusation about my behavior -- I'd made advances toward a girl when she was home alone. The high schooler was the accuser.

Thankfully, Mindy had been with me when we stopped at the girl's house. She'd picked out the magazines. Not only that, but we'd gotten stuck in traffic on the way to her house, and we'd seen Pastor Rick stuck a couple of cars away. We'd all waved to each other. I reminded Rick of the incident, and he knew the charge was baseless.

That probably would have been the low point of that year -- if it wasn't also the year the church fired me. I can't say I did a good job that year, but it would have been tough to do much at the church at that time. Not many years later, the church died.

Anyway, apart from time spent with my brother's family and a few baseball games, most of my memories of Minnesota were not fond ones, but we still had to go back to the state because that was our job: visit every state, even ones we'd never wanted to return to.

***

To be honest, we were looking forward to some things in Minnesota. My brother and sister-in-law and some of their adult kids live in the Land of 10,000 Lakes, and we were looking forward to time with them. The beds were always more comfortable than the tent floor or van seats. The food was better than BK or Wendy's. And conversation was easy. We enjoyed time with old friends and new friends, but the family time was some of the most cherished on the trip.

My brother, Daryl, works for the Evangelical Free Church of America at their headquarters outside the Twin Cities, and we happened to be there for the annual meeting of GlobalFingerprints, a branch of the Free Church's international outreach.

Most people are familiar with the child sponsorship programs of such organizations as Compassion International, Save the Children, World Vision, and others. We've seen the commercials with children with very big eyes and bigger needs. Like those organizations, GlobalFingerprints (GF) links sponsors with children.

In Haiti, where unemployment was nearly 90 percent and many parents weren't able to care for their children, GF has made the strategic decision to focus on children who live with at least one parent. With the help of sponsors, the children can continue to live with their parents while GF helps provide food, clothing, and resources for education.

One member of the GF team told about putting together a Haitian teen band. An announcement on Minnesota Public Radio brought in enough money to purchase instruments for an orchestra. In Haiti, knowing how to play an instrument can make it possible to find work performing at weddings and funerals.

Another GF worker told about a summer program at a beach resort usually reserved for foreign tourists. While students and adult leaders spent time together in a beautiful place, the teens were gaining leadership skills to help them succeed as adults. One church in Illinois provided the essential items the teens would need: towels, bathing suits, and sandals (things most of them had never owned before).

In different parts of the world, GlobalFingerprints has different methods. In Liberia, they work with orphans -- children who lost their parents to the Ebola epidemic of 2014 and 2015. Some of the work takes place on Peace Island, which sounds picturesque until you learn that the island's surrounded by swampland. Many of the children live with relatives who need financial help to provide even minimal care.

India offered special challenges. In spite of ongoing need, India's government limited Western funding. Christian charities weren't the only organizations banned; even the Gates Foundation was prohibited. Still, some work was able to continue, including feeding children who live in a garbage dump.

In that one morning's meeting, we also heard about GF's work with children and families in Congo, Indonesia, Lebanon, Myanmar, Panama, and Zambia. During our year on the road, we spent a lot of time talking about how the Church did a good or bad job caring for people in America. It was good to have this reminder that the Church does so many good things around the world.

***

When we looked back at our year of living in Minnesota, we remembered good things along with the bad. We lived in one of our favorite apartments, in the same building where Mary Richards of *The Mary Tyler Moore Show* lived. That neighborhood was full of fun restaurants and stores (and a couple of bars). On this visit, after looking at all the old familiar places, we found a new place, and it was one of our favorite bars of the trip.

Amanda, the bartender, was very excited that she'd discovered a set of brain-shaped gelatin molds. Who wouldn't be excited? Brain shaped strawberry gelatin might be just what somebody needed to distract a zombie in a life-or-fate-worse-than-death situation.

Distracting zombies, killing zombies, hiding from zombies -- these topics were never far from the minds of customers and staff while we were in Donny Dirk's Zombie Den in downtown Minneapolis.

Just to be clear, Donny Dirk's Zombie Den was not a safe haven for zombies. Instead, it was intended as a safe haven during a zombie apocalypse. During our trip, *The Walking Dead* still led the Nielsen ratings, and two zombie films (*Pride and Prejudice and Zombies* and *Scouts Guide to the Zombie Apocalypse*) were released. There was even a zombie app ("Zombies, Run!") which encouraged fitness through zombie phobia. The excesses of zombie mania in our culture didn't make Donny Dirk's any less delightful.

Nothing about the exterior attracted attention, which was just as well. If it were too shiny, it might lure the undead. The interior, on the other hand, was decorated with all kinds of grotesque knick-knacks and memorabilia. Weaponry was available behind glass cases if ghouls came a-knocking, including a chainsaw. The men's room had a collection of shanks as an inspiration for other do-it-yourself weapons. ("Hey, I could whittle my toothbrush into an instrument of death!")

The music playing wasn't strictly thematic, though I did hear the Ramones' "I Want to Be Sedated" which seemed apt. The TVs played horror related offerings: the British animated series *Duckula* and the TV miniseries adaptation of *It*.

The drink specials were horror themed, too. I had a Slackjaw and Mindy had a Dead Russian. Our drinks were tasty, but some of the offerings on the menu were less appealing (to us, anyway). To promote an upcoming event, the Minneapolis Zombie Pub Crawl, many shots were mixed with Red Bull.

Because of the unique setting, we changed out our usual questions, asking instead, "During a zombie apocalypse, what might be the advantages of going to a good bar?" and "What about a church?"

Tammi, the bartender, noted the many advantages of coming to Donny's: the double doors at the entrance would be helpful for getting people in but keeping zombies out; she pointed out the weaponry (including a machete I'd somehow overlooked.) "This would be one of the safer bars." She noted they had MRE's available for a zombie siege. She hoped a church that fed the homeless might have plenty in stock when the eventual and inevitable uprising of the dead occurs.

Kelly, another bartender, hoped the holy water and Crucifixes would be handy if the zombies called in vampire reinforcements. He also said,

"Maybe if you have faith, you know, it would be better for keeping your peeps together."

We met a couple at the bar, Evan and Hannah. They were students at the University of Northwestern-St. Paul, a Christian college, so we wondered if their responses to zombie questions would have more theological depth. Evan cited bars' advantage of "flammable liquids available" for fighting zombies with fire.

Hannah said, "If you're doomed and you're not going to survive, you could get super drunk so that the end wouldn't be so terrible."

As for a church, Evan mentioned that some churches had a lot of entrances and exits which might be a disadvantage because there'd be so much to seal off. He said his church had "an underground, easily fortified space," and mentioned that churches tended to have tools which could prove useful. He also noted that some churches had broadcast facilities, which could prove quite useful.

Hannah thought a church "could be a place of comfort in an otherwise uncomfortable time."

As we philosophized on the subject, Evan said, "If I could choose how God would end the world, it would be a zombie apocalypse." We speculated on whether the Book of Revelation could be interpreted in that way but came to no firm conclusion.

We asked Amanda, the finder of the brain molds (and a manager), the same questions. She noted that Donny Dirk's would be a particularly good place to hide out if George Romero's vision should take place. "This building is an old structure; it's a safe haven. Once those doors are locked, you're safe. There's not a lot of food, but there is food. Even if you have to survive on olives." She also said the people who choose to get very drunk could be used as zombie bait if it came to that. Bartenders would be survivors in such conditions because they're used to "multitasking in chaotic situations." She thought that even if a church had food, "the stained glass would be extremely fragile."

At different times during the evening, I remembered a youth group event I'd organized, a zombie night with undead costumes and games. Kids posted photos, which led to an email (not from a parent or anyone from the church) chastising me about the evils of exposing children to the Satanic influence of zombies. I responded that we'd used the night to introduce a discussion of Ephesians 2:1, where Paul wrote that we were dead in our sin, contrasting that state to new life in the resurrected Christ. She didn't write back.

We'd finished our drinks, but Tammi told us we shouldn't leave before the 11:00 pm laser light show. We stayed, and we were glad we did. Strobes and laser lights shot around the bar (some appeared to come out of the eyes of mounted deer heads). We were so happy we made it to Donny Dirk's, and we were sad when we recently heard it's no longer around.

***

While we were in Minnesota, we got to thinking that sometimes it's a good thing for a church to die. As I mentioned before, my year serving at Central Evangelical Free Church in Minneapolis was a miserable one. After the church died, the building still stood.

Central Evangelical Free Church was founded in the 19th century by Swedish immigrants. Through the years, the descendants of those founders moved into the suburbs, but the families commuted in for church on Sundays. As the years went on, the church's vision and purpose became less clear. Attendance dwindled. Discontent grew. An offer to buy the church building was voted down by a narrow margin.

As Central died, Hope Community Church was being born. At first, the new congregation met at Stadium Village Church near the University of Minnesota, but the two churches grew to the point that sharing space didn't work anymore (which was a good thing). Hope began to look for new facilities.

The congregation's leaders got together with the Evangelical Free Church, and, instead of selling the building, the Free Church gave it to Hope Community Church. The death of Central Evangelical Free Church allowed Hope Community Church to grow and thrive. They grew to a point where they needed more space, and a neighboring Lutheran church offered to sell their former building for what it had cost them in the early 1900s.

Hope Community Church continued to minister to University of Minnesota students; half of the congregation were students, and many graduates who stayed in the area also stayed on as part of Hope.

Being back was strange. The sanctuary looked pretty much the way we remembered it -- probably like it looked a hundred years earlier. The gym, the kitchens, the classrooms, and even the restrooms were all where we remembered them, but the art on the wall and the people in the building were not what we remembered. I'd been on staff with a senior pastor, a church secretary, and a part-time choir director. Hope Community Church, according to the photos on the wall near the sanctuary, had several pastors and a whole flock of interns who were studying both the practical and the academic aspects of ministry.

Nathan Ziegler, middle school principal during the week greeted us at the sanctuary door. As we chatted, he told us about his website,

"Minnesota Cold!" which features experiments conducted in the depths of frozen Minnesota winters. Network news shows, the BBC, and (naturally) the Weather Channel had featured his experiments.

Nathan, a graduate of the University of Minnesota, first attended Hope twenty years ago. He wasn't a Christian then, but a dorm mate brought him to church. Nathan came to Christ and stuck with Hope. I asked Nathan what attracted him to the church on those first visits, and he said the leadership and the people were "real and down to earth." I asked if that was still true and he said, "That's why I'm still here."

We talked with Jill Chimieleski, whose husband is senior associate pastor. She said students talk about Hope being a "duct tape church" -- the church wasn't perfect, but people weren't perfect either, and it was good to patch things up together as you went along until the Kingdom comes.

During worship, Joel, a staff member, spoke of the importance of communion and connectivity in the church. He mentioned his irrational fear of zombies and asked people to share an irrational fear they had with someone seated near them. (I still don't understand why Joel called fear of zombies irrational.) I liked the idea of encouraging that kind of vulnerability.

The music was a blend of old and new. We sang hymns of Watts and Wesley with electric guitars. The sermon was about the Crucifixion, so the worship team performed Cage the Elephant's "Shake Me Down" during the offering. It wasn't a match I'd have ever thought of, but it certainly worked.

We happened to be there the first Sunday of the month, the week Hope celebrates communion. As songs were sung, people went forward for the bread and the cup (grape juice) when they were ready. One of the songs, sung to the tune of "Auld Lang Syne," had powerful lyrics, and it was good to hear a good tune revived, just as we appreciated the revival of the old building.

In my time serving at Central Free, there didn't seem to be much concern for the community surrounding the building. The people of Hope, on the other hand, care for the poor and disadvantaged in the neighborhood surrounding the church's buildings by partnering with established programs in the area (such as New Life Family Services, Prison Fellowship, and Big Brothers and Big Sisters) rather than creating their own programs.

Our week in Minnesota felt a lot like a circle of life, and though we were sad to learn that a good (zombie) bar had died, we were thrilled to know that a place of worship had been brought back to life.

12
THE BLAZING SADDLE

"You've been to forty states, and this is your first gay bar?" Bryan, one of the owners, asked incredulously. It was a pretty good question.

We hadn't planned to visit The Blazing Saddle that night in Des Moines. We'd looked up another bar that looked interesting and had very cheap drinks, but when we looked inside, no one but the staff was there. We thought it was odd for things to be so quiet downtown on a Thursday evening (Weekend Eve), but we suspected that a whole lot of people were at the Carrie Underwood concert at nearby Wells Fargo Arena.

(Carrie Underwood was a continuing presence on the trip. In Tahlequah, Oklahoma, we bought pizza where she once worked. In Hawaii, we heard about her filming a scene in *Soul Surfer* where she quoted from Jeremiah. The director asked her to do a take without the Bible verse, and she refused. And here she was again.)

So we walked to the state Capitol building and took pictures of the statues and the sunset. We wandered past stores that had closed an hour or more earlier and looked inside one or two more nearly empty bars. Then we came across The Blazing Saddle, where business was bustling. Inside, the bar was pretty full, and there were even people outside having a smoke.

We went in because there were people to talk to, but I also found the name of the bar attractive. I love the early films of Mel Brooks, especially that great five film streak from *The Producers* to *Silent Movie*, with *Blazing Saddles* smack dab in the middle.

One of the bartenders, Christopher (he's also an owner), greeted us cheerfully when we sat at the bar. Christopher is big on welcoming. Sometimes, he told us, if he sees a regular approaching while he's smoking outside, he'll toss his cigarette in the ashtray so he can hurry to greet them and get their drink. "You can't let them wait at the bar," Christopher said. He sometimes went through a pack a day like that. Mindy asked Jesse, the man next to her, what he was having since she thought chocolate might be involved. He told her it was a coffee martini and offered her a sip so she could decide if she wanted to order it (He'd mentioned the drink used tequila, and Mindy wasn't sure if she'd like it). She declined the sip but ordered the drink when he said it tasted like mocha.

They started talking, and Jesse said he worked in human resources, and he told us horror stories about customer service. We then asked him our two standard questions, "What makes for a good bar?" and "What makes for a good church?"

To the first question, Jesse said, "My answer has changed as I've gotten older. If I had to pick a word, I'd say 'relaxed.'" When he was younger, he liked loud places with as many people packed in as possible. He said now he likes a place where he can talk with people and enjoy some music. He said that at The Blazing Saddle, "Anybody's welcome here." As for a church, Jesse said, "It'd have to be open and affirming. So for here (Des Moines), that'd be Plymouth Church." Jesse added, "I grew up Pentecostal. I don't like it where the format's all rigid." He joked about churches where "you have to stand up at 9:04 and sit down at 9:05, the same time every week." He also likes "a positive message and not fire and brimstone." Until he left his hometown to go to school, he'd often led music in his church, and he misses it. "Music in church is unifying. It's the closest thing to real magic the world has."

I was next to Joe, and he was alongside Jim, his partner of thirty years. The bar's been around for thirty-three years, and they'd been frequenting The Blazing Saddle for most of those years. Joe said, "We like this bar. People know each other. It's a family atmosphere." He said the bar serves good strong drinks, though he sticks to beer. He said he wants a bar to be welcoming, clean, comfortable, and safe; he implied The Blazing Saddle hadn't always been that kind of place, but it was now. Joe talked about the good things the bar does, such as collecting toothpaste and soap for people living with AIDS and the homeless. The bar has raised money for LGBT students through Bingo, drag shows, and silent auctions.

I asked Joe what would make for a good church. He said, "They should have activities that keep you interested and bring you back." He said a church didn't have to be a hundred percent supportive of the gay movement, but they shouldn't be "preaching against the gay world." He added that a good church, like a good bar, should feel like family. Most churches he'd known had been warm, and he thought a church should be a place where you could socialize without being judged.

The crowd had thinned a bit, so Mindy asked Aaron, another

bartender, our two questions. He said a good bar needs a "combination of staff and clientele. We have regulars creating an atmosphere of enjoyment; we're the Cheers of Iowa. We treat people the way they want to be treated. And I should add that we have the strongest, cheapest drinks in the state."

Aaron said a good church needs "an understanding of who your people are, who's coming in." He said it should be a place, in the words of his grandmother, where "whoever walks in your front door is family. Welcome everybody who comes in." He argued the Blazing Saddle is kind of like a church, "but our communion is fireballs and peppermint shots. People come in here to get the stress of the world off their shoulders. Religion and bars are two entities that do that same kind of thing. There's a lot of sin in here, maybe, but a lot of charity, too. If we have a show, it's for a good cause, like for veterans. It's one of the things we're known for around here."

Just outside the front door, we had another chance to talk with Christopher, who was smoking on one of the benches. He thanked us for coming, and we took the opportunity to ask our two questions. For a good bar, he said the primary thing is "a good, stiff drink." But he clearly thought a good bar needed many other important qualities, and that The Blazing Saddle reflected those qualities. He said their bar is "friendly and not threatening, whether you're straight, gay -- whoever you are, you can come in and have a good time."

We told Christopher how we'd appreciated his friendly greeting when we entered, and he said, "If you own a business, you have to be that way." He said that's how he's been since he entered the service industry at the age of 14.

He hesitated about answering our church question. "My parents were hippies, so I never grew up with religion. I didn't grow up with church. I never went to church." As a kid, he went to church weddings and funerals and Vacation Bible School in the neighborhood. He said his "other half," Matt, grew up Catholic but doesn't go to church anymore. He and Matt sometimes go to a straight bar near their home. One of the owners, a Catholic woman, used to lecture them on their lifestyle until Christopher asked her, "Who are you to judge me?" After that, he said they'd worked through their differences and had become friends.

Bryan, another owner who'd been working behind the bar, joined us and teased us for not going to a gay bar earlier. He said The Blazing Saddle had won so many awards in the local papers for best neighborhood bar that they'd considered changing the award name to "The Blazing Saddle Award." When he told us they have regulars who've sat in the same seats for years we weren't surprised that Bryan referred to their place as the "Gay Cheers."

Especially since we had a great time and we were made very welcome, I guess I need to answer Bryan's question, "What took us so long?"

***

It's childish and petty to try to assign blame, but it was mainly Mindy's fault. Way back in February, in New Orleans, I'd suggested going to a gay bar, but Mindy said no. When I asked her why, she said she was concerned that we'd go in viewing people as "The Other" rather than as people. She also said, "People aren't going to a gay bar to meet an old couple like us."

She admitted she was also concerned about going to any bar where the focus was on sexuality and seeing things she'd have a hard time unseeing. We'd avoided some straight bars that had a reputation for being pick-up joints. There are places where the, um, entertainment is rather explicit and we preferred to avoid those places.

***

Even though we hadn't gone to any gay bars, we'd gone to gay-friendly churches. One of those churches, Saint Gregory of Nyssa Episcopal Church in San Francisco, had been part of our preliminary church visitations in 2015 because author Sara Miles ministers there.

In the opening paragraph of her book, *Take This Bread: A Radical Conversion*, Miles introduces her tale of a remarkable, virtually instantaneous work God did in her life. She describes herself as a leftist, radical, lesbian atheist who, in a simple encounter with Jesus through the bread and cup of communion, changed into a very different person: a leftist, radical, lesbian Christian.

We'd loved our time worshiping at St. Gregory. During our year of traveling the United States, we went to services at Episcopal Churches and other mainline Protestant denominations that have made a point of publicizing their inclusiveness.

When I talked to some of my evangelical and fundamentalist friends, they questioned whether people are the Christians they claim to be if they're unwilling to submit to obedience to God and His Word in the area of sexuality. Other friends have said that judging or condemning people for their sexual identity or sexual choices is not Christlike.

During the trip, we stayed with my two best friends from seminary. Both pastors, they've taken opposite positions on same-sex marriage. Their views of church and Scripture obviously shaped their opinions. One friend, Rob Merola, was pastor of Saint Matthew's Episcopal Church in Sterling, Virginia. He stressed that a good church should be welcoming, with authentic spiritual life. Not everyone has to be on the same page (he noted an agnostic who was a regular attendee), as long as everyone is moving in the same direction. People should be learning to live sacrificially, and the church should provide people with a sense of accountability. A good church should have a real impact on the community and the world (not just by writing checks, but through authentic relationships).

Rob said he believes the Episcopal Church has an advantage over many evangelical churches because it doesn't promote a false sense of adequacy: the Episcopal church takes Scripture seriously, but doesn't approach it as a rulebook for proper behavior. He is comfortable with the denomination's support of same-sex marriage and the ordination of gays and lesbians.

Our other friend, Steve Palm, was pastor of Geneseo Evangelical Free Church in the small town of Geneseo, Illinois. Steve has a passion for languages, not only studying Hebrew and Greek during his school years but Aramaic as well. While preparing a sermon, he examines texts in the original languages. When we stayed with him and his family, his love of the people of his church is quite apparent. I talked to Steve about the story of Sara Miles and people we had encountered in our travels who have reconciled their Christian faith with their homosexuality. He worried that people become inoculated from true Christianity by exposure to an amorphous Christian faith that omits anything difficult or challenging from the Word of God.

Frankly, the conflict on these issues in the church provided a fair deal of cognitive dissonance during our travels. We talked to many people who answered the question, "What would make for a good church?" with, "being open and accepting, particularly of the LGBTQ community."

What seemed strange to me was that we heard this mostly from straight people. It was hard to imagine that answer would have been so common in straight bars even ten years ago. I think it's good that people want to be considerate of people different from themselves, but it is an interesting social phenomenon. I couldn't help wondering if the attention these issues have received from the media over the last few years was the primary reason for their answers. They weren't asking, "Is a church opening and accepting of single people?" or "Is the church opening and accepting of those with disabilities?" The church has problems with these communities as well. But responses to our question of what makes a good church often focussed on acceptance of the LGBTQ community and concern about the church's stance on same-sex marriage.

I certainly don't believe churches that take a stance against same-sex marriage necessarily do so from ignorance and prejudice. Churches must honor the words of Jesus, and He said in Matthew 19, "Have you not read that He Who made them in the first place made them man and woman? It says, 'For this reason a man will leave his father and mother and will live with his wife. The two will become one.' So they are no longer two but one. Let no man divide what God has put together." We said that during this year of cross-country travel we would only go to churches that honor Jesus. To me, that seems like a real tension for a church to honor both the teachings of Jesus and same-sex marriage. How is it possible for churches to hold such very different positions on this issue?

Throughout the trip as I puzzled over this conflict, I was encouraged when I turned to the tiny New Testament book of Philemon. It reminded me that controversy is not a new thing in the Christian Church. These days, there is widespread agreement in the Church that slavery is wrong. Every church we visited would certainly give slavery a big thumbs down, but that wasn't the case in New Testament days when slavery was generally accepted as a natural and acceptable institution of the world.

The book of Philemon is a letter named after its recipient and written by the Apostle Paul. Paul wrote, "I always thank my God as I remember you in my prayers because I hear about your love for all His people and your faith in the Lord Jesus." This Philemon sounds like a pretty great guy; the Apostle Paul himself has a high opinion of the man.

The thing is, he's a slave owner. The whole letter is Paul encouraging Philemon to free a slave, Onesimus. But Paul, regardless of Philemon's response to his request, never casts doubt on Philemon's Christian faith.

I was encouraged by two stories we'd heard about ministries that approached LGBTQ issues from very different stances.

In Washington D.C., we visited an independent church that has a more inclusive view of sexual orientation. The church's mission statement called people to become authentic and thoughtful followers of Jesus and to join God in the renewal of all things. We heard about a gay man who attended the church without his partner. We'll call them James and Carl. Carl assumed the church James attended would be judgemental of them and their relationship, so he avoided the church.

James was hit by a car. He went into a coma. Whenever Carl visited James in the hospital, he would always find someone from the church there as well. People from the church prayed for James and assured Carl there was hope. In time, James came out of the coma. The church continued to rally around the couple. Carl enthusiastically joined James as part of the church where they felt supported as a couple. This church clearly demonstrated the love of Christ.

Another story came from a rescue mission where a different stand on this issue was taken, yet Christ's love was just as clearly demonstrated. The pastor was preaching through one of Paul's lists of sins. One of the sins on the list could be interpreted as "homosexuality." The pastor was teaching that we all sin, and homosexual acts are sinful; a sin like jealousy and coveting and lying and gossiping and all the other things that all humans do. All humans sin and need God's grace and forgiveness.

A man in the congregation stood up and began to yell at the pastor. "How dare you judge my life like that?" As a gay man, he felt the pastor was attacking him. The pastor thought he had acknowledged he wasn't pointing to one sin but was making it clear that everyone sins and needs Jesus. The man said he would report the pastor to his superiors. The pastor was actually a little amused by this. The mission was sponsored by the Southern Baptists, and the pastor thought he presented the issue in a much more liberal fashion than might be found among other members of the denomination.

But the story didn't end that night. The man started standing outside the mission and as people came for meals and services he would yell, "This place teaches hate!" He stood outside shouting for weeks, then months. He wasn't always there when people came, but he kept coming on occasion.

After several months, the pastor heard that the gay protester was having a hard time paying his gas bill and, as they say in the north, winter was coming. The pastor found the man and told him, "We'd like to pay your gas bill. Understand, this isn't quid pro quo. You can keep protesting and yelling at people and telling them we preach hate if you choose. We just want to pay the bill."

The man accepted the offer. And though it wasn't asked for, he quit protesting in front of the mission. After a few weeks, he came back to church and told the pastor he was now gay and celibate. The pastor told him, "Whatever. We're just glad to have you back."

That rescue mission and The Blazing Saddle both welcomed us graciously. I believe Jesus would feel at home in both places as well.

13
Ominous Phone Calls

We were on a winding two-lane road through the Black Hills of South Dakota that occasionally narrowed to just one lane. Dark was coming, but there was enough light to appreciate the green meadows, the trees, and the railroad tracks that were sometimes by the road, sometimes above it. We mostly knew where we were, though our connection to Google maps was spotty.

Eventually, we drove into a tunnel through a mountain pass. At the other end, we saw Mount Rushmore framed by trees and catching the sunset glow. It was jaw-droppingly beautiful. While our year-long expedition was about visiting bars and churches, sometimes we looked at the gorgeous countryside and thought, "Wow. Maybe this is what this trip is all about."

We'd spent several frosty nights camping in Nebraska the week before, and it was time to pack the tent away. We found a motel in Rapid City after stopping briefly to admire Mount Rushmore in the chilly twilight. The next morning, refreshed by sleeping in a motel, we decided to take a side trip to Deadwood, figuring we'd spend the night in the minivan -- until we saw billboards for $20 hotel rooms. It turned out there wasn't a catch, so we enjoyed a comfortable night in a historic hotel.

Melody, the bartender at the No. 10 Saloon didn't wear a gimmicky old-timey costume, although a variety of other folks we saw in Deadwood did. She was wearing a black T-shirt with a camo hoodie, and she welcomed us with genuine hospitality and good humor.

"You have to read people," she said. "You figure out if they want things straight or if they're just looking for a good story." Melody has lots of opportunities to tell stories about her bar, the Saloon #10, infamous for being the place Western legend Wild Bill Hickok was shot dead by Jack McCall while playing poker.

Thousands of tourists come through the small town of Deadwood every year to relive the history not only of Wild Bill, but also the woman who claimed to be Bill's sweetheart, Calamity Jane, and learn more about Teddy Roosevelt's good friend, Lawman Seth Bullock. (These stories gained a renewed currency with the HBO show, *Deadwood*, which we watched while in the state.)

Melody told us that afternoon at the No. 10 is tourist time, especially during the summer when daily shows featured Wild Bill shootouts. Even on a Tuesday in October, when we visited, there was an afternoon show. The tourists are usually on a tight schedule, making a quick stop at the No. 10 after viewing a stunt show in the street, then off on to Mt. Rushmore. Melody said the evenings bring a different crowd, more casual tourists, serious drinkers, and locals.

Melody liked to tell people, "Wild Bill used to sit in that chair by the fireplace. I'm not making any promises, but people have taken pictures of that spot and had unexplainable ghostly images appear in their photos."

She told this story to a group of tourists. One elderly woman returned after the group left, screaming and pointing at Melody, "Liar! You liar! The stories you told me are not true!"

Of course they weren't true. A look at a historical marker across the street informed us that the original No. 10 Saloon where Hickok was killed in 1876 was burned down (along with most of the town) in 1879. Today's No. 10 is across the street the original location. You almost wonder whether the chair displayed above the bar door, the one where Wild Bill was sitting when he was shot, is the genuine article.

As the reporter explains in John Ford's classic western, *The Man Who Shot Liberty Valance*, "When the legend becomes fact, print the legend." (Did I mention we saw a statue of Ford in his hometown of Portland, Maine?)

While we chatted with Melody and another bartender at the #10, Lia, we asked them our two questions, "What makes for a good bar?" and "What makes for a good church?"

Both agreed that in a bar the staff sets the mood. Melody said she likes "a feisty person who can do some back and forth with the customers; a little sassy." Lia agreed that the feistiness was helpful in dealing with customers who'd had too much or tried to make advances. They mentioned the delicate balance required to turn down those advances without losing out on tips.

Lia said a good bartender knows when customers want attention and when they want to be left alone. She added that years of bartending should earn a person a degree in therapy.

I asked what made for a good church. Melody said, "Non-judgemental is a big one for me. People shouldn't go into a place and feel out of place for being a sinner." She said it helps "to at least have a buddy to go with." She admitted she doesn't go to church because she and her boyfriend sleep too late on Sundays.

Lia said she goes to church and, in fact, teaches Sunday school. She described her small church as nonjudgmental. "It took me a long time to find a church that was okay with tattoos." Her position as a bartender and Sunday school teacher had its advantages, she said. "I've got people to go to church with me because I work at a bar that might not go otherwise."

Since we'd most recently lived in California, the idea of churches that wouldn't accept people because of their tattoos was strange to us, and it seemed even more foolish since one of the best sermons we heard on the trip was from a tatted-up preacher in Nashville.

***

We left Deadwood and booked a room in a Rapid City motel through Sunday. We'd found a church meeting in a mall that had a Wednesday night Bible Study, so we decided to go. On our way, Mindy's phone buzzed.

It was her dad. Since Mindy's parents rarely called -- and never midweek -- we were alarmed and pulled into a fast food parking lot to take the call.

It was bad news. Mindy's mom had gone to the hospital for a check on stomach pains. Her doctor discovered an abdominal mass; surgery or treatment wasn't an option.

Mindy asked, "How long?" Her dad said the doctors thought it was a matter of weeks, not months.

We didn't go to church that night after all.

***

Back at the motel, we tried to plan. Our first concern, of course, was Mindy's folks, but we were also, frankly, thinking about what this meant for our trip. Would it be best for Mindy to fly home immediately and stay with her mom? Sure, it would be the end of our quest, but in the grand scheme of things, how much did our trip matter?

As we talked, we realized that our trip did matter. At least a little. To us. Our location complicated things. On the map, we were in the big empty area where Southwest didn't fly (we didn't have money for a flight, but we did have just enough points). The next three states were the opposite direction from the airports we needed. Until we got to Colorado, nearly a month away, we couldn't figure out any way we could keep our project alive and go back to Indiana.

Mindy checked on flights from Denver, and we hoped and prayed that her mom had enough time left.

***

Within a few days, members of Southport Presbyterian Church surrounded Mindy's dad with support. He asked several godly women, friends from the church, to sit with Marilyn for an hour each day, and Mindy's sister Jennifer drove from northern Indiana to be with their parents.

We were still in Rapid City, South Dakota, where we couldn't help with the situation in Indiana, so we stuck to our routine. Our hotel had cable, and TCM (formerly Turner Classic Movies) happened to be playing *North By Northwest* (we'd brought the DVD along since we'd planned to watch it as our South Dakota film, but this was easier).

Historic Elks Theater (where they had the genius promotional idea of "Bring Your Own Bag Night" for popcorn) was playing *Priceless*, a film about human trafficking (you know, to cheer us up). Even without the Wednesday night service, we managed to visit two very different worship services that week.

Friday night we drove 45 minutes north to the Filling Station in the small city of Sturgis. We could see the large white cross from the highway (the cross is illuminated with red lights at night). We found the narrow parking spaces, intended for motorcycles, even more interesting.

Bill and Jeri arrived after we did, but we were extra early, and they were delayed by a flock of bighorn sheep in the road (and traffic for a Kenny Rogers concert in Deadwood).
We asked about those motorcycle spaces in the lot, and they confirmed that bikers are a big part of their summer ministry. Since 1938, Sturgis has hosted a major motorcycle rally, and most of the stops have been in small-town bars -- except the stop at the Filling Station, also known as The Mission at the Cross.

Bill and Jeri serve in all three of the ministries that call the Mission at the Cross home. First, there's the Filling Station, the worship service held most Friday nights. Then there's Hellfighters, an evangelical ministry with events for bikers that included prayer tents that offered the hope found in Jesus. Finally, the ministry worked to meet the needs of the community through things like toy drives and free oil changes for single moms and others struggling financially.

The ministries also worked to reach outlaw bikers (the 1% who participate in criminal activity). In the past, such groups have helped with the Mission's toy drive (I was reminded of the TV show *Sons of Anarchy*), and some outlaw bikers have come to faith in Christ.

A few days later, still hoping we were making the right decisions, we made it to Rushmore Mall for Sunday morning worship at Hills of Grace Fellowship. We thought its location, next to the At Home store, was appropriate. Feeling at home seemed to be an important element of going to church for people we were talking to at bars wherever we found ourselves.

That afternoon, somewhere on the drive to Minot, North Dakota, Mindy's phone died for good. Months before, in Florida, the phone's screen had gotten cracked. The crack had grown over time, leading her to find workarounds rather than spending the money to replace it. We weren't just concerned about staying in touch with Mindy's dad; she could use my dumb phone for that. But we depended on her phone for GPS, especially because we didn't have a paper map of North Dakota and only a general idea of the roads we needed to take. We got more nervous as the sun went down because my phone started getting road closure alerts related to protests on the nearby pipeline.

***

We made it to the Minot area an hour or so after dark and found a convenient Walmart parking lot for our last night of sleeping in the minivan. Corinna, a friend from Minneapolis days who'd been too young for youth group (her older brothers had been regulars, though) would be meeting us the next afternoon. She and Mindy had been friends back then, and we'd loved the family.

Corinna had arranged for us to stay in Almont, a little town half an hour west of Minot/Bismarck, at a relative's hunting retreat (it was called the Sunflower Inn, but there were a lot more pheasant feathers and box elder bugs than there were sunflowers). It was a charming town, but my phone didn't have any reception. For the next few days, until it occurred to us to ask Corinna for the Wifi password, we spent a lot of time in the Minot public library. Thankfully, we were able to order a new phone and have it delivered to Corinna's house, and my phone worked in the library parking lot, so we were able to stay in touch with Mindy's dad.

Once we got settled in, we got started on our North Dakota activities. Looking back, in spite of our anxieties about Mindy's mom and communication difficulties, it was an oddly satisfying week. We drove two hours to visit a bar that claimed to be the geographic center of North America (Hanson's, in Robinson) where they were experimenting with a pumpkin cannon in preparation for the Halloween party that weekend.

After everyone in the bar trooped out to watch the pumpkin shot from the cannon (it didn't quite work), we all went back inside. After everybody had settled down with their drinks, I took advantage of the break to ask Courtney the bartender our two questions. She said that for her, a good bar had a relaxed atmosphere, good selection, and friendly people. As for a good church, "I was raised in the church, but

I don't go anymore. The church kicked me out because I didn't look right."

I was confused by what in Courtney's appearance could offend. As far as I could tell, she looked like a stereotypical farm girl with blonde hair and a bright smile. After a moment, though, I realized that much of her upper chest was tattooed, so I asked if that's what she meant.
She said it was, then added, "Churches need to understand there's more than one way to be a Christian."

I was furious at the anonymous church leaders who took it upon themselves to decide some ink should keep Courtney out of the gathering of Christ's Body. I'm still angry when I think about it.

***

It was a relief that the two North Dakota churches we visited didn't seem to be places that would kick someone out because of tattoos. We found out about them because Rodney, a cowboy poet, stopped by the Sunflower Inn to find out about the strange, bumper-sticker covered van parked on Almont's main street. (I guess it's true that there are no secrets in a small town). Rodney told us there was a church we needed to see.

Back in the 1990's, Rodney was driving home from a rodeo in Wyoming when an unexpected blizzard hit. He and other travelers found shelter at Assumption Abbey where, at the time, the monks raised cattle. It was calving time, and Rodney (who's also a rancher) helped deliver a couple of calves. He's remained friends with some of the monks and told us we needed to visit the Abbey.

"It isn't far," he said, "Forty or fifty miles." (We noticed distances are viewed differently in different states. People in, say, Vermont, might think of that distance as an all-day outing; in North Dakota, fifty miles is a pleasant little drive.)

So on Saturday morning, we drove to the Abbey (changing from Central to Mountain Time on the way, though we were still in North Dakota). The door of the visitors' center was locked, but a couple toting some of the Abbey's wine told us the monks were all in the church for a worship service. So we went to St Mary's, the church associated with the Abbey, to worship with the monks.

When the service ended, one of the monks stayed to tidy up. After we introduced ourselves, Father Odo invited us to join him for lunch. Father Odo's parents were married at St Mary's, he was christened and had his first communion there, and he has served at the abbey for the last 57 years as a member of the Benedictine Order.

When we asked him what he'd done there, he pleaded laziness, but then mentioned he'd been the Abbey's business manager and a pastor to the community. He worked binding books, was a key maker, and taught music. The day we met, as on most days, he was the organist. So...he did a few things in those 57 years.

The next morning we walked to the worship service at the United Lutheran Church of Almont, where we realized we were sitting behind Rodney and his family. At the potluck lunch after the worship service, we enjoyed talking with people from the town where we'd been living that week.

***

Earlier in the week, on Wednesday, we'd picked Mindy's new phone up at Corinna's house. She'd missed a call from her dad, but even back at the Sunflower Inn, we didn't have the reception to call him back. In spite of our reluctance to impose further on Corinna's hospitality (and that of her relative, who had so kindly allowed us to stay at his place), Mindy called her dad on the landline in the Inn's kitchen.

Dad said that her mom had died a few hours earlier; that he'd been with her; that she'd died peacefully and without much pain. The next day, he called again to let us know that the memorial service would be in a little more than a week, on a Saturday.

So we headed east instead of west after church on Sunday.

***

We spent the night at my brother's in Minnesota, where we'd been just a few weeks before. The next morning, we hurried through Wisconsin and Chicago to spend the next night with Mindy's sister Jennifer and her husband Mike in West Lafayette, Indiana.

Their kitchen was full of food brought by their church small group. We knew Mike appreciated the really big box of Cap'n Crunch cereal, which he loves but doesn't often buy. Some items were for us to share with Dad, so we found room behind the driver's seat and headed the hour-and-a-half south to his apartment.

We spent the next few days sorting photos, packing up clothes and other incidental belongings, running errands, and meeting with the pastor of Southport Presbyterian Church to discuss the memorial service. Mindy's dad had served that church as senior pastor for around 20 years until his retirement (it's also the church where we were married). Dad had already done much of the planning for the service, and Jennifer had spent hours making sure details of the service were according to his and Mom's wishes.

***

The memorial service was scheduled for 2:00 pm that Saturday, with lunch at church for the family before people began arriving. Mindy was especially touched that part of that lunch was fried chicken from a family friend who'd remembered her childhood complaint about finding the fried chicken gone after she waited politely (as instructed by her parents) at the end of the line. This time, she could have all she wanted.

Mindy's mom, Marilyn, hadn't been able to attend church for several years before her death, and it had been 20 years since her dad's retirement. Still, scores of church members and friends lined up to greet the family, sign the guestbook, and participate in the worship service. Mike and Jennifer's pastor and several members of their small group had driven from West Lafayette for the service. Several members of Mike's family, as well as their son-in-law's parents, drove in as well.

A man at a bar had once told me that the best thing about a church was having a place where people would care for him when he was old and ailing. He thought of it as an investment, like a IRA, but instead of putting in money for a future payments, you invested time into a church that would pay off later. People would give you their time when you really need it. For Mindy's parents, that's definitely how the church community cared for them.

Southport Presbyterian's senior pastor introduced the memorial service as a time of worship for the risen Lord Jesus Christ and as a time to honor Marilyn Date, Mindy's mom. Scripture readings and hymns connected the memories shared by three members of the family (and one dear, long-time friend who'd served as associate pastor when Mindy's parents first arrived at Southport Presbyterian).
I've noticed that memorial services in a church often have a certain tension concerning the purpose of the gathering: is it primarily a worship service to honor God, or is it mainly a time to honor the person who has died?

At one church where I served, a beloved, integral member of the congregation passed away. His mother was adamant that the service should honor Jesus, and that there really didn't need to be any mention of her son in the service. The pastors reminded the mother that many of her son's friends would come to the service expecting to honor her son -- but the mother had a point as well. If Jesus truly offers hope of life after death, that hope is something grieving people need to hear about. Mindy's dad decidedly wanted to honor Jesus by highlighting our hope of eternal life with Him, but he struck a balance between that and honoring Marilyn's life.

After going to church with Mindy's dad on Sunday morning, we hit the road again so we could reach our friends in Colorado on Election Day.

14
SCUM OF THE EARTH

 On the two-day trip from Indiana to Colorado, we decided to make a tourist stop in Abilene, Kansas, to visit Dwight Eisenhower's Presidential Library, childhood home, and grave. It was also election day. Mindy and I have rarely missed an election, but we didn't have an address, so we'd decided not to register to vote. Still, through most of the year, we'd paid close attention to the campaigns.

During the year, we'd talked with people who supported the different Presidential candidates; to keep those conversations friendly, we didn't talk about who we supported -- which was easier to do as the year went on. Frankly, the leading candidates didn't excite us greatly. On Election Day, though, we decided to make a bold, public, political statement. At the Presidential Library gift shop, we bought an "I Like Ike" bumper sticker and added it to the collection on the back of the van. We have yet to regret the decision.

***

Our destination that night was Dave and Becca's home. They'd co-pastored our church in Healdsburg, California. The TV was on when we arrived, and the election returns played through dinner and all evening long. Though Dave and Becca tried to keep politics out of their ministry, I knew they had been enthusiastic supporters of President Obama. Needless to say, that election night was very difficult for them, particularly for Becca. Considering the work she does, her distress was understandable.

Becca is one of the most loving, caring people I know, and she feels things deeply, which is one of the reasons she's so effective in ministry. As the president (and, she jokes, janitor) of Charizomai International, the non-profit she founded, she serves women in prison, refugees in the United States, children in Gaza who've suffered from continual fighting all around them ("Definitely the scariest place I've ever been," she said. "If the border closes, you can't get out."). In all her work, she cares for those who've suffered great pain and trauma, sharing the love of Christ through word and deed -- from hugs to hospitality.

During our visit, Becca was preparing for a trip to Uganda to work with children alongside local ministries. (One of those ministries was Sports Outreach, a recreational and educational organization featured in the Disney film *Queen of Katwe*, which we'd seen at the Fleur Theater in Des Moines, Iowa.)

***

Where do you start when you're trying to help children move through the suffering and difficulties of their lives toward a healthy future? If you're Becca, you begin at the Dollar Tree store.

By using art and play therapy (with supplies from Dollar Tree), children -- and adults -- can safely express their experiences, enabling them to heal from past trauma.

Becca told us about a child who drew pictures of children. In drawings with a sunny sky, the children looked sad. The children looked much happier in drawings of cloudy, rainy skies. Becca asked the child about the drawings; she found out that on sunny days, the village was likely to be bombed.

When Becca had visited Gulu, Uganda, the year before, the team had helped over 300 children from area villages. One group of 75 had traveled in a dump truck. Most had walked, some without shoes, to Gulu for the week-long camp.

Some of the children Becca worked with had been abducted and forced to serve as child soldiers in Joseph Kony's Lord's Resistance Army. Some of those former soldiers now serve as local leaders and pastors; they share their stories to help others realize that God has better plans than what they've experienced in the past. By being open even about their own past horrific acts while currently living lives that demonstrate God's love and forgiveness through Jesus, these leaders encourage others to accept that same love and forgiveness.

Becca told us, "A lot of times, it just helps to have support. The biggest thing is getting supplies to the kids." The supplies, ranging from balls of yarn to playdough, filled the two suitcases Becca was taking to Gulu. The support she mentioned is less easy to pack. She can ask for financial help, but she trusts God for the emotional, physical, and spiritual strength the ministry and travel requires.

As we watched election returns, we realized much of her work is with refugees, many of whom hope to come to the United States someday. Candidate Trump had talked a lot about immigrants. Her concern was understandable.

Two days after the election, another woman in Christian ministry expressed a very different point of view.

"I once had a woman on a tour who had been helped by counseling service," Betty, the Focus on the Family tour guide, told us. "She told us that she had been considering taking her own life. As a nurse, she knew the drug and the dosage she could take to make her death look like a heart attack. Just before she took the drugs, the phone rang. It was a counselor from Focus on the Family." The woman had asked for prayer a short time before. The counselor on the phone referred her to a counselor close to her that she could meet. Her life was changed for the better. That's why she wanted to visit Focus on the Family Visitor's Center."

We wanted to visit Focus on the Family because I knew they stocked the children's books I wrote, the Bill the Warthog series. Like bookstores in general, Christian bookstores are vanishing in America, but the bookstore at the Focus on the Family headquarters in Colorado Springs has a large and varied selection, particularly for children. I asked one of the clerks if I could sign my books (we'd brought a Sharpie along just in case), and she let me. I also told her about our project of visiting a church and a bar in every state and our intention to write a book about the trip.

She said she'd love to read the book. She added that it probably wouldn't get stocked in that bookstore. The bar aspect would be a problem.

After we visited the bookstore, we thought we should take the tour. As we got started, Betty told us that two hundred thousand people visit the facility in Colorado Springs every year. We appreciated the opportunity to be among them.

Focus on the Family was founded in 1977 by psychologist James Dobson to support families. Their most prominent ministry, the radio program, airs five days a week and explores parenting, relationships, sexuality, and more from a conservative Christian perspective. More than 2,000 radio stations in North America carry the program, and through that ministry, people are encouraged to contact the organization for help of various kinds -- like the nurse who asked about counseling.

In the past, psychology has been regarded with suspicion by many churches and Christian ministries. Focus on the Family has helped many conservative Christians get the counseling help they need.

In 1981, Dobson founded another organization, the Family Research Council, which is a political lobbying group for conservative causes. Dobson and the Family Research Council have primarily supported the Republican Party since the organization began. Legally speaking, The

Family Research Council and Focus on the Family are separate entities, but through the years they have shared personnel and values.

After our tour, we asked Betty how we could pray for her and for the ministry. She suggested we could pray for Focus on the Family's effectiveness in the aftermath of the election. With their conservative stance on social issues, particularly regarding abortion and issues related to gender and sexuality, the organization has proved controversial through the years. Betty made it clear that most people at the ministry were pleased with the result of the Presidential race, but were concerned about ongoing political friction in the country. She suggested that they wanted to continue to minister to a wide variety of people, but the increasing divide in the nation made that challenging.

Just as I could understand why Becca was upset by Trump's victory, I could understand why Betty was relieved by Clinton's defeat. The concerns, the fears, and occasionally the hopes of people across the political spectrum was something we'd observed in red and blue states.

***

Early in the trip, and while the primary season was in full swing, we spent time with a seminary friend who unexpectedly found herself in the midst of a national political kerfuffle. Kathi DeCanio works at a very cool ministry called IHOP (it stands for International House of Prayer, and a legal scuffle with International House of Pancakes is part of their history). IHOP Kansas City (to distinguish from the place with syrup and bacon) was founded in September of 1999, and since then, worship and prayer have been continual (all day, all night, 365 days a year).

Kathi's boss, Mike Bickle, founded the ministry. Shortly before we arrived in Kansas City, Bickle privately gave his support to Presidential candidate Ted Cruz. His support was personal, and Bickle didn't intend his support to become a public endorsement on behalf of the International House of Prayer.

After someone in the Cruz campaign leaked Bickle's support, some in the press began to research Bickle (for "research" read "muckrake") to make Bickle look like a crazy person tied to Cruz. Anyone who preaches in public can have things taken out of context to make them look crazy. As a Charismatic Christian, Bickle (like many other preachers in that branch of the Church), often spoke biblical prophecy related to the "end times."

Some in the church see Israel's 1948 founding as a fulfillment of Scriptural prophecy and part of God's plan for the world. MSNBC used a clip of Bickle discussing this in a sermon, where he said that God used the horrors of Hitler and the Holocaust for His own purposes.

A fairly universal teaching in all monotheistic religions is that God can turn bad things into good (as Joseph says in Genesis 50:20, "What you meant for evil, God intended for good."), but MSNBC commentators claimed that Bickle was pro-Hitler and pro-Nazi. It was just crazy talk, but while we were there, Kathi was doing her best to help Bickle use social media to respond to the accusation.

While we were staying with Kathi, a few days after this, another event (the death of Supreme Court Justice Antonin Scalia) caused the news to drop that scandal for new ones.

***

The whole incident reminded me of the potential toxicity of mixing church and politics, but you can't keep the two apart. In the current climate, politics is on many people's hearts and minds. And people should be free in church to bring their real concerns.

At a Baptist church we visited, I was playing pool with high schoolers before youth group when one of the guys asked me who I'd be voting for. I told him I was just as incapable of voting in this particular election as he was.

"If I was able to vote," he said, "I'd be voting for Donald Trump." (At that point in the year, I wasn't taking the Trump candidacy seriously. Even though I thought he was serious about his run, I didn't think he had a chance of winning the Republican nomination. Maybe I don't have a future in political punditry. Of course, none of the pros seem to get it right either.)

I asked the kid why he liked Trump; he said, "He's the smartest guy that ever ran for the Presidency. He's rich. That shows he's smart." I thought about noting that Hillary Clinton wouldn't need to be applying for Welfare anytime soon, but I changed topics. That was, though, the first of many times I was taken by surprise to find such enthusiasm for Donald Trump's presidential run.

We heard a very different view of Trump when we visited another

Baptist church, 16th Street Baptist in Birmingham. When we toured the mini-museum in the church's basement, along with photos and displays celebrating the Civil Rights movement, were photos and displays celebrating Barack Obama's Presidency. Though many Republican candidates were still actively running at that time, I heard negative remarks at the church about only one: Donald Trump. Looking back, I wonder if Trump was the one candidate members of the church were concerned could win the Presidency.

That was one of few times during the year we heard partisan politics discussed from the pulpit. During a sermon reminding us that we should expect trouble in this life, Reverend Price said, "You may lose your job! One of your children could get hooked on drugs! Donald Trump could be President!" That last line got a big laugh from the congregation; it seemed like such an unlikely thing.

Earlier that morning, in the Sunday School class we visited, the election had also come up. Most people in the class seemed to favor Hillary Clinton and were concerned about Donald Trump. After some fretting, one man settled the conversation by saying, "No matter who is President, Jesus is King!"

***

Bars were also usually politics-free zones. More than once, people described a good bar as, "A place where they don't talk about politics or religion." Still, not everyone felt that way.

At The QuarterDeck in Long Beach, Mississippi, we'd hoped to watch the Warriors' basketball game. Oddly enough (in a sports bar, anyway), the largest, central screen was playing a Republican debate, and it seemed to be getting more attention than the sports on the other screens.

It wasn't exactly respectful attention, though. Someone yelled out, "They're like two-year-olds. It's great!"

Someone else said, "Don't change the channel...They might break out in a fist fight!" It was hard to believe that the debate was winning any votes from those bar patrons that night.

A TV at Tom's Old Bogies in Wisconsin led to a very different discussion later in the year. When Hillary Clinton appeared onscreen, she was greeted by a chorus of boos from the crowd at the bar. One of the men asked if anybody had seen the roadkill deer nearby. He said somebody had put a sign on it, "He was going to vote for Hillary but we took care of it."

Driving through Michigan and Wisconsin, we were surprised to see more Trump than Clinton signs. Predicting elections by campaign signs in people's yards isn't exactly science, but it made us less surprised later when we saw those states change from Blue to Red on election night. Even after the election, we saw and heard starkly contrasting attitudes toward the results. When we arrived at our motel in Vernal, Utah (populated by dinosaur statues), in mid-November, the motel clerk asked, "What do you think about the new President?"

I grunted something noncommittal.

"It's great to have a businessman in the White House," the man behind the counter continued. "I think he'll really turn things around."

It seemed he thought Trump would turn things around for the better, but I'm not sure. I wasn't looking for that conversation. We'd been driving all day, partly on a gravel road while racing the sunset through an insufficiently mapped area. I was looking for a bed.

***

A few weeks later, we stayed with Christina, a high school friend, in Boise. Her husband has health concerns, and she was terrified that the

new administration would lead to the loss of their medical insurance. In Idaho, we also heard praise for the President-elect from the pulpit at Sanctuary Cowboy Church.

We were a little disappointed that there were no horses in the parking lot of the church, though most of the

men wore cowboy hats that they removed during prayer. The church didn't meet out on the range somewhere, either, but in a strip mall in a suburb of Boise.

Nonetheless, the interior of the church, from the worship center to the restrooms, were decorated with Western themes, including faux trees (well, some of them were Christmas decorations), fences, saddles, lariats, etc.

We'd first met members of a Cowboy Church at the start of the trip, and we'd seen Cowboy Churches from Arizona to Kansas and from the Dakotas to Montana. If for no other reason, we felt we needed to visit a Cowboy church to balance our visit to the Indian Baptist church in Oklahoma. (At that church in Tahlequah, the capital of the Cherokee Nation, we heard scripture and hymns in English, Cherokee, and Choctaw). Sanctuary Cowboy Church, though, had a family connection. The pastor, Keith Brown, is my nephew's wife's uncle. So he's kind of kin.

You might be wondering what makes a Cowboy Church a "Cowboy" church. Here's what we found out: for one thing the music has a country western/old-time gospel feel. Keith said most who attended his church are farmers and ranchers. People in his church get together for horseback rides and skeet shooting, and the church sponsored gun safety events to help people in the church earn conceal and carry licenses. They've also sponsored CPR lessons and fundraising events for Life Flight Network (which provides emergency medical transportation).

On our visit, Pastor Keith was preaching on Advent but often wandered off topic ("I just wanted to tell you that because it's a good story," he said at one point.) Near the end of the sermon, Pastor Keith encouraged people to pray for President-elect Donald Trump "whether you like him or not" because he would have authority over a "Christian nation."

Pastor Keith's request has Biblical support, First Timothy 2:2, where Paul encourages readers to pray for those in authority. But Keith went on to say, "Trump has said he's going to use his own jet airplane rather than Air Force One and save us all kinds of money. He's accomplished a lot more as President-elect than that other guy did in eight years in office." (I assume by "that other guy" he meant Barack Obama, though he might have meant another President. For example, James Monroe and Ulysses S Grant served two terms as well.) This church seemed to be serving their targeted group well, but if I were the pastor there, I'd leave the politics out.

***

Back in Colorado on the Sunday after the election, we worshiped in a church where I'm pretty sure people would have voted Blue, but they left politics out of the service that evening when emotions were high. That church was Scum of the Earth.

From the outside, it was a traditional-looking downtown church, more or less. When I came through the door into the building, I had to dodge a little kid dashing around the corner. I heard the sound of a pinball machine and followed it to find two boys fighting over the flippers. A plastic children's slide was set up (and in use) in the worship area, and the wheelchair acce3ss on the side of the room was being used as a ramp by a kid in an office chair. The worship service hadn't started yet, but once the service began, quite a few children started dancing in the open space at the front, near the worship band. One little girl elegantly practiced what I'd guess were moves learned in her ballet class. Meanwhile, much younger kids spun around and fell down. I guess what you should know is that Scum of the Earth is a kid friendly place.

The name of the church comes from I Corinthians 4 where Paul
describes himself and his coworkers as "fools for Christ...We are
cursed...We are persecuted...We have become *scum of the earth*." The
congregation's founders purposely chose a name that didn't sound like
a church; they wanted to reach people who wouldn't usually feel
comfortable in church.

There was a smoking porch out front, where a staff member was the
designated smoker, hanging out with anybody who dropped by and
going inside only when it was time for the sermon. As in everything
else, the goal was to make people feel welcome and comfortable
enough to go inside. Punks, skaters, ravers, the homeless, and whoever
else could be found on the streets of Denver were welcome. (I would
guess that a Venn diagram of these groups and Trump voters would
not have a lot of overlap, but the diagram on the church's website
doesn't directly address politics.)

Fran Blomberg, one of the lead pastors and the evening's preacher,
gave several of us visitors a tour after worship. After the church bought
the building from an eccentric artist in 2008, it took a year to get
everything up to code, particularly the restrooms. We were pretty
amazed by what's been done there in the way of painting and
refurbishing (one bathroom has a display of painted toilet seats, another
has walls covered with pennies), but the whole place still has a scruffy
feel. Along with more traditional sanctuary decorations, hubcaps and
bikes are displayed in the worship area. And all of the scruffy, offbeat
elements are intentional, though not necessarily planned, to help people

on the fringes feel at home in the church.

During the service, the political situation came up. The theme of the worship service was obedience, and while introducing the prayer time a man said, "We pray for our nation. We have elected new leaders who may pass new legislation that might make us need to decide whether to obey the laws or obey God." In the concluding time of prayer, people were encouraged to hold hands. I took Mindy's hand, and the man next to me offered his wrist, covered by his jacket sleeve.

Free dinner with potluck elements followed the worship service. As we enjoyed spaghetti, salad, and rolls, it was easy to forget the turmoil of the week which had followed the election. As we had been reminded in Birmingham months before, "No matter who is President, Jesus is King!"

15
WINTER IS COMING

Throughout the year, we often chose the church we'd visit because our friends went there. That was the easiest way to choose. Sometimes, we found a church with historical interest or a unique ministry. Montana might be the only place we chose a church for its location.

We knew we needed to get from whatever church we visited in Montana to Twin Falls, Idaho, by 6:00 pm Sunday night. A winter storm was expected in western Montana on Sunday afternoon. The Dodge Caravan had been trustworthy throughout the year, but we didn't want to put it -- or ourselves -- through any dangerous weather situations, especially in isolated areas. Driving in a snowstorm through a mountain pass was a whole other thing from driving on dry, level roads, and we didn't want to do it if we didn't have to. We stayed with friends in the shadow of the Bitterroot Mountains for a few days but decided that the closer we could be to the Idaho border for Sunday morning, the better.

***

We didn't know anybody in Dillon, Montana, but the location was ideal. We even got to enjoy the town Christmas party on Friday night, when Santa Claus and carolers roamed the streets, stores stayed open with hot cider and cookies to tempt shoppers, and little children tried to figure out if they liked being out after dark. We felt right at home.

On Sunday morning, during the worship service at Dillon Assembly of God, the snow started swirling around outside. Mindy fought the temptation to suggest leaving before the service ended, while I felt responsible for the service starting late.

Neil, who led the worship service, had noticed the minivan, and we'd gotten to talking about the trip. Though nobody seemed to mind (maybe they didn't even notice), the service started late as a result. Then during the announcement time, Neil asked us to tell about the trip. I kept thinking that maybe the service would have been over before the snow started if I hadn't talked so long.

We learned that this little church was celebrating -- they were expecting a new pastor to come before the next week, and they'd been without a pastor for nearly half the year. As they praised God for His provision, we were reminded we could trust Him to get us through any nasty weather to come. (Or to not get us through, if that was what He wanted.) So not only did we stay through the whole service, we chatted with people for a little while after.

In spite of our concerns, the storm, at least where we were driving, didn't amount to much. We knew worse weather was likely to be ahead of us, but we made it to Twin Falls in plenty of time.

***

A flier didn't quite make it to the trash, which probably changed everything. Kaishon, a high school senior, thought the free ballroom dance class it advertised, at Xrossway Fitness Center, sounded interesting, so he went the next Monday night. He joined the gym, which led to attending Xrossway Church. On his 19th birthday, he was

baptized at the church, and the night we visited, Kaishon taught the ballroom class.

I know that might sound a little confusing, but Xrossway is a fitness center and a church. The year-old endeavor was the vision of Clint Lutz, a Lutheran pastor and church planter we'd met while he was serving a church in Healdsburg. Since moving to Twin Falls, he and his wife Bonnie had spent two years raising financial and personal support while preparing to open the gym/church.

I asked Clint about his fundraising pitch for the combination gym and church. He said he started with Mark 12:30, "You shall love the Lord your God with all your heart and soul and mind and strength" because he wanted to build a ministry to the whole person. Many gyms say they're designed to build the whole person, but Xrossway actually hopes to do it.

The gym and the church, two separate entities, work together. Clint said he hopes the fitness center will eventually provide the church's financial support so that all church offerings can go to local needs and missions. He felt that church plants could no longer count on financial support from outside as denominations decline in strength.

Becoming a vital and helpful part of the community is a significant part of the church's vision. According to Clint, every church should ask the question, "If we were gone tomorrow, would the community miss us?" Too many churches only interact with the community when they're asking people to come to their fundraisers.

So the Social Monday ballroom dance classes are free (other dance classes charge a fee). A different health and fitness class is available to the neighborhood free each month, and they have a goal of providing 20 percent of their gym memberships free to people in need ("free" could also mean bartering a service in exchange for a gym membership).

We had fun in the dance class, though Mindy just observed most of the time. She'd fallen while sliding on the ice in Hannibal, Missouri, back in February and didn't trust her knee when the dance required swiveling. Kaishon did a great job with the class, demonstrating steps with amusing patter.

We stayed in Twin Falls for two days, and I was grateful to be able to use Xrossways' fitness equipment. We'd stayed at a few motels with fitness rooms or pools, and I'd taken long walks when I could through the year, but I was glad for the chance to exercise after spending so much time behind the wheel.

We were a little sad we couldn't attend an actual worship service at Xrossways because we had other friends to visit in Idaho. Nonetheless, we were glad to see what the church and the fitness center are doing to make the people of Twin Falls more whole.

That desire for helping the whole person had reminded us of a ministry at First Presbyterian Church of Fort Smith, Arkansas, where we'd visited in February. That church, with a big, downtown edifice and a congregation who mostly lived in the suburbs, had wanted to do something to help their neighborhood, so they got in touch with a nearby junior high.

When the church found out that the cheerleaders didn't have uniforms or mats to practice (safely) on, they offered to help if the cheerleaders would donate time at the church. The arrangement worked so well that the cheerleading squad won the state championship. We got to attend the celebration dinner the church threw in their honor where it was apparent that the relationship between the squad, the school, and the church was becoming a firm bond, to the benefit of the community and the glory of God.

From Twin Falls, we drove to Boise. Overnight storms left the ground covered with several inches of snow, but snowplows, sand, and salt were doing their jobs. So far, the van was holding up to winter.

***

In spite of money and weather concerns, we appreciated that the last month of our trip, in spite of money and weather concerns, was mostly spent with old friends. We'd been looking forward to going to an Idaho bar with Christina, a friend of mine from high school, since long before the trip began. We stayed with her and her husband, Tom, in Boise, reminiscing about the time we'd co-starred in the play *Stage Door*.

Our characters were supposed to kiss, but we were so awkward that the director had said, "Maybe you could just hug." A few years later, I left theater behind, but Christina made it into a career. Tom was also an actor who'd taught high school drama for many years and had been a regular at the Idaho Shakespeare Festival.

They'd suggested going to Pengilly Saloon. A local environmental group was sponsoring an event that night, and by giving them our email addresses, we each got a free drink. The downside was that the bar was crowded and there wasn't room at the bar. Instead, we found a booth, which proved to be the perfect place to ask our friends our bar questions.

Christina said, "It really is who you're with at the bar." She shared some fond bar memories, including some from the bar we were in. Pengilly's was the place the Idaho Shakespeare Festival company met after shows, and after the May through September season ended, friends from the company continued to get together at the bar. The dance floor was tiny, but the troupe would crowd onto it, and Christina and Tom said they enjoyed watching the pros dance.

Christina mentioned other bars that held fond memories. While dating, they'd gone to Tom Grainey's Sporting Pub, a favorite spot for local bands. When they requested a ballad, the band dedicated John Coltrane's "Naima" to them. For the next couple of years, whenever Tom and Christina went to the bar, that band would strike up "Naima."

Tom said a good bar was "just this loud. I like to chat more than dance."

Both agreed they appreciated a good jukebox. "I like it when they play Johnny Cash -- even though I don't like Johnny Cash anywhere else," Christina said.

Christina mentioned just one word to describe a good church, "Joy." She grew up attending a small Baptist church with her parents, and joy was lacking. She quit going to church as soon as she was free to do so. (Another time she had told me about a lively African American church she'd encountered on a theater tour. She wondered whether church might still be a part of her life if she'd grown up in a church like that one.)

Tom hesitated about answering the church question because, after years of struggling with the issue, he had finally decided to go from labeling himself an agnostic to calling himself an atheist.

I said that we'd talked to plenty of atheists on the trip who had ideas of what churches should be like, and after a time, Tom said he appreciated when a pastor is a good storyteller. He said his first wife was more religious than he was, and he used to sometimes go to her church. The pastor of that church was very good. Tom appreciated those messages, and Christina confirmed he still quoted that pastor. Tom also said. "I love Christmas music; I love holiday music. That spectacle of it keeps my nostrils above the water for the rest of the year."

We knew what he meant. As the winter got going, we were finding hope in the thought that Christmas -- and the end of our journey -- was coming too. Throughout Utah, Wyoming, and Montana, we'd enjoyed looking at snowy fields and mountains while listening to Christmas CDs we'd packed just for this month. (If you've never tried singing along with Bob Dylan's gravelly voice on his Christmas album, you might need to try it -- though we can't honestly recommend the album.)

***

After visiting the Cowboy Church in Boise, we headed west. We spent the night in a motel just over the border of Oregon, state 49, before heading for Bend for a day with another high school friend. The snow on the trees and fields had an icy glaze that sparkled in the sunlight. It was amazingly beautiful, but we were grateful the snow was on the fields and trees rather than on the road.

As we loaded the car in Bend, we heard we'd definitely need chains over Mount Hood on the way to Portland. We hoped we'd heard wrong.

Mindy had bought the chains when she took the minivan in for its last oil change before the trip, back in December of 2015. They'd been neatly stored behind the driver's seat for almost a year, and whenever we noticed them, we were torn between thinking it would be nice if we didn't need to use them at all and feeling like we'd wasted money on them if we never took them out.

About halfway to Portland, as we climbed the eastern side of Mount Hood, the dilemma was resolved when lighted signs announced "chains required." We pulled over.

I hadn't tried this set of chains, and it had been years since I had installed any. I looked around at the truckers pulled off just ahead of us, trusting their superior road knowledge, but upon observation, some of them seemed to be cursing at their own tires and just as uncertain as we were.

Mindy got behind the wheel, and I got on my back in the snow beside the tires. I got the chains on, though we weren't entirely sure they were secured. We drove slowly up one side of the mountain through gorgeous, terrifying, snowy woods, over the top, and headed down the western slope. After an hour or so of very slow, very nerve wracking driving, we could remove the chains, which had managed to stay on the whole way.

***

A different kind of snow storm raged (briefly) indoors at Capernaum Club in Portland. Club members and leaders wadded up paper towels into snowballs and threw them at each other. Blake Shelley, the leader of the club, seemed to take the most "snowball" abuse, but he accepted the hits cheerily.

I've led and participated in many such activities at Young Life Clubs (a non-denominational Christian outreach that mostly serves adolescents). I was part of a club in high school and led other clubs in college and seminary. Most of what we did at Capernaum's Christmas party were activities I'd seen at other Young Life Clubs: games, skits, singing, and a message; the difference in this group had to do with the students involved. Capernaum Young Life Clubs minister to teens and young adults with intellectual and developmental disabilities.

Blake Shelley, from his wheelchair, greeted leaders and students as they arrived. (People seemed especially happy to see Blake's service dog, Stanley.) The big screen TV was playing *A Charlie Brown Christmas*, and decorating Christmas cookies was the first activity of the afternoon. Everyone went to work applying frosting, though many cookies were eaten before their aesthetic worth could be fully appreciated.

I asked different kids what they liked about Club. Marcus said he liked the chance to hang out with his friends. Victoria said that she loved camp, leading other kids to say they loved camp the previous summer or to anticipate going to camp that summer.

Most summers, Blake takes the club to Washington Family Ranch, a camp in the high desert of Central Oregon owned and operated by Young Life. Capernaum students usually have individual counselors that look out for them at camp, but the week also allows them unique independence, excitement, and fun.

After eating way too many frosted cookies, the group was divided into two teams to turn leaders into Christmas light-covered trees. Mindy and I had the honor of judging the competition -- we enjoyed getting to declare one team the winner, but it was less fun to admit one team hadn't won.

Blake screened two JibJab videos. First, Santa's reindeer with leaders' faces danced a Yuletide Macarena, then rampaging carolers had students' faces. Both videos received great snorts and guffaws of recognition.

We sang Christmas Carols including "All I Want for Christmas" (the Justin Bieber version), "Jingle Bells," "Away in a Manger," and "Joy to the World." One of the students, Jeffrey, kept requesting "Jingle Bell Rock," so Blake relented and said we could sing it at the end of Club. At the close of the club, Blake gave a talk (as he does toward the end of almost every club gathering). Because Blake has cerebral palsy, his speech can be difficult to understand, so one of the other leaders "translated" Blake's talk. Blake replayed Linus' reading of the Christmas story from Luke to remind the group what Christmas is all about. He expanded on the message, "This is the coolest thing. God came into the world to have a relationship with us." Club ended, and farewells were said, with the promise to get together again after the holidays.

The next day Mindy and I had breakfast with Leonard Shelley, Blake's dad and a friend of mine since elementary school. He told us that when he was driving Blake home from high school one day, Blake said, "Dad, I know why God made me this way."

This got Leonard's attention, and he listened as Blake told him that having cerebral palsy would let him share Christ with other people with disabilities.

***

We'd been looking forward to getting to see our Oregon movie, *Loving*, at The Living Room in downtown Portland. We'd heard there was a winter storm on the way, and while we were in the theater wet, sleety

snow began to fall. We'd paid for our minivan to stay in a lot all afternoon, so in spite of the threatening conditions, we decided to see a couple of important tourist destinations in Portland: Powell's Books and Voodoo Donuts. I added to my odd collection of paperback novelizations of '70's and '80's sitcoms (*Happy Days: The Bike Tycoon* and *Welcome Back Kotter: The Sweathog Newshawks*), and we picked up that night's dessert for dinner with seminary friends -- Froot Loop and Cap'n Crunch topped donuts.

Getting out of the parking lot was tricky since the pavement under the fresh snow was icy. The nine-mile drive to our motel took an hour and a half, and as cars swerved and traffic stopped on the snowy road, we debated calling to cancel dinner. But we hadn't seen Jan and Fran for nearly thirty years, and we didn't know when we'd have the opportunity to see them again. We went, and while we were eating dinner, the snow stopped. By the time we left their house after several hours (we were so grateful to spend that time with them), the snow-covered roads were empty, but the storm had ended.

***

The next morning we were on the road south to Medford. The streets were plowed, but we saw at least twenty sets of chains that had apparently been poorly attached to tires. We were relieved that we'd made it over the mountain and through the storm safely.

On the road south, we listened to an old radio broadcast of Dickens' *A Christmas Carol.* We were struck when Bob Cratchit said about his sickly son, Tiny Tim, "Somehow he gets thoughtful sitting by himself so much and thinks the strangest things you ever heard. He told me, coming home, that he hoped the people saw him in the church, because he was a cripple, and it might be pleasant to them to remember upon Christmas Day, who made the lame beggars walk and blind men see." Sometimes, people feel uncomfortable seeing disabled people, and some churches just don't do disabled ministry well. Bear Creek Church in Medford, where we were headed, was different. Another old friend of mine, Dale Meador, was the pastor.

At church, we met Rachel, whose son, Bryce, is in a wheelchair. She told us about visiting a church with her son. She was told, without apology, that their Sunday school was downstairs, and nobody even suggested any accommodations. At some churches, she said, they've just been ignored.

Bear Creek is not that kind of church. Signs outside assure families that people with disabilities and children are welcome.

Dale, his wife Nancy, and I attended the same church in San Diego back when I was a student at San Diego State University. Dale taught the college Sunday School (he was just a couple of years older than most of us, but being married gave him a distinction in our eyes). Ten years ago -- nine years after Dale planted the church -- Bear Creek Church began to focus on special needs after connecting with Joni and Friends, an international ministry caring for those with disabilities. Nancy, who struggles with chronic pain and also works with a non-profit that provides physical and occupational therapy for children, first made the connection.

The church website gives fair warning that during the service you may hear yelps or screeches from, say, young people with autism. Toward the end of the second Sunday service, while a video was playing, a little girl wandered on the stage and walked back and forth a bit, stopping to pat the speakers. Nobody seemed bothered because, in this church, it's not a big deal. Bear Creek Church takes Jesus' admonition to let the children come very seriously.

The Sunday we visited, Dale definitely wasn't preaching that God will give you material wealth and health if you do the right things. Instead, he focused on the connection between Christmas and suffering. Christmas teaches that through Christ, God didn't promise to prevent suffering, but He promises to be with us in the midst of suffering. The meaning of "Emmanuel" is "God with us."

Dale had asked us to share a bit about our year's adventure in both services. He used our experience as perpetual first-time visitors to encourage people in the congregation to welcome people and show interest in them. "Tell me about yourself" was what Dale encouraged his congregation to say to others at church they didn't know.

Bear Creek Community Church rented meeting space in a school, requiring regular setting up and tearing down chairs, sound equipment, and signage. After the service we watched several children stacking chairs until they heard they didn't need to because of the school's Christmas break. (I remembered when Dale and I attended San Diego Community Church, we met in a YMCA. Chair setup and teardown was a weekly ritual.)

During one of our conversations the church's ministry, Dale said, "Families with special needs really need the church, but churches also really need families with special needs."

I'm sure Tiny Tim would agree. Tim thought seeing a lame child would remind people of the one that healed the lame. As Paul wrote in II Corinthians 12, it is through weakness that Christ's power can be seen. So yes, the church needs special needs.

After lunch at a Mexican restaurant with Dale and Nancy, Rachel, Bryce, and her husband Brent, we headed toward California. A little snow had fallen recently, and we were concerned about the last mountain pass on I-5. We really didn't want to use the chains again, and sometimes the pass is closed.

We breathed a sigh of relief as we crossed into state 50. The sky was blue and the only snow we could see was on Mount Shasta.

16
HOME

I was born in California. Even during three years of seminary in Illinois and the year I worked at a church in Minnesota, I still visited the state a couple of times a year. This trip was the longest I'd ever been away -- 356 days. When we began the journey, we thought we might fall in love with another state. In a few places during the year, we thought, "We could live here." But when we crossed into California, crossing the border, we felt the relief and joy of homecoming.

In every state we'd had a checklist of things to do: church visit, bar visit, movie theater visit, watch a movie and TV show from the state. The first item each week, though, was to cross the state line. As we left Oregon, we knew that even if we swerved off the road, tumbled down a mountainside and exploded into a gasoline-soaked fireball, we'd made it to all fifty states during the year.

On Sunday night, we checked into a motel in Redding. The next day we planned to drive to a bar in San Francisco -- another item to be checked off our list. As we approached the Bay Bridge, the odometer on our van hit 200,000 miles.

***

In spite of our fears throughout the year, it was a little easier to keep going because we'd told a lot of people about our plans. Among those I'd told were Tim Goodman and Jason Snell, co-hosts of the podcast *TV Talk Machine*. Tim is the chief TV critic for the Hollywood Reporter, and Jason produces the program (which is "released simultaneously worldwide" every week to an untold number of faithful listeners).

In Nevada, I'd tweeted to them about watching an episode of *Crime Story* set in Las Vegas. Tim and Jason read that tweet on the podcast. From then on, I let them know what state we were in and what show (set or filmed in that state) we were watching.

A couple of months into the year, Tim expressed doubt that we were actually traveling. I couldn't blame him, really. After that, I started adding photos to my tweets when we visited TV-related sites (like Niagara Falls, the setting for *Wonderfalls*, the Mary Tyler Moore statue in Minneapolis, and of course, the entrance to Cheers in Boston), with the TV Talk Machine logo in the shot. After a while, convinced we were traveling, Tim speculated that our travel budget must be exorbitant. I refrained from tweeting a photo of us camping at Walmart.

Sometime midyear, Tim and Jason mentioned that a meetup for podcast listeners might be fun. I wrote in to ask if the event could take place the Monday before Christmas. They decided on a San Francisco bar, The 21st Amendment, and announced the meetup on the podcast.

It turns out, a bar in a business district can be pretty busy on a Monday evening.

Another TVTM listener, Matthew, arrived when we did. When we asked the hostess where the private party was, she sent us to the upstairs room. That room was full of young people dressed for a night on the town, which didn't seem like our group. Mindy said backless dresses were a sure sign of a holiday work party, not a TV podcast meetup.

We went back downstairs and, along with a few other TVTM listeners hovering near the entrance, staked out a couple of small tables and some space at the bar. Before long, Tim and Jason arrived, and all sixteen of us crowded around four small tables.

I was surprised by how little of the conversation was about television. At times some of us launched into lengthy diatribes about the podcast or our interests or pet peeves, and Tim and Jason listened patiently. I appreciated their appreciation of their fans.

We had fun meeting others who'd had their messages read on the podcast. Several men named Allen like to argue with Jason; collectively, Jason calls them his nemesis. One of those Allens was there, and it turns out, he's a great guy.

I had a great time talking to "Kate from Rwanda," who had indeed traveled from Rwanda for the meetup (and, I'm sure, for Christmas with her family). Kate works with the United States consulate in Rwanda specializing in literacy issues; when we met, she was struggling to find a Rwandan author who could write children's books.

We'd been asking the same questions at bars all year, but it seemed like a good time to go with something different. We asked "What TV bar do you remember?" and "What TV church do you remember?" Kate refused to be constrained to a literal interpretation of the question. She chose Monk's Cafe from *Seinfeld* -- not a bar but a place people gathered to eat and talk. (Kate is not big on sticking to the choices offered. We asked people to choose from a list of California TV shows to decide what we should watch. She wrote in her selection, *The O.C.*)

Kate's mother, Kristen, had come along to the meetup. She said the hospital chapel on Showtime's *Nurse Jackie* was memorable: "Where people went when struggling with existential issues, a sanctuary." Mindy asked "Design Geek Jess" our questions. Like so many others over the year, she mentioned *Cheers*, but the church she remembered was from *The West Wing*: President Bartlet's "Hamlet moment" in the National Cathedral in Washington, D.C.

Mindy asked Thom the same questions, and he thought of Moe's Tavern from *The Simpsons* and the church from the final episode of *Lost*, saying "it was really heavenly." He spoke admiringly of Glide Memorial, a real church in San Francisco which he said is "not just for people who believe. The way they sing and the way they present the message is incredible." He appreciated the work Glide had done for people with AIDS/HIV.

"Nemesis Allen" also said *Cheers,* "though in a real bar you're more likely to be surrounded by people who aren't friendly." I asked if there were a TV church he'd like to attend, he said that was unlikely as he's an atheist. "When I see churches on TV, I wonder what's motivating them from a plot perspective. I assume there's something nefarious going on." Allen mentioned AMC's *Preacher*, which certainly has nefarious things going on, but said that show got too weird for him.

I asked our host Jason about his favorite TV bar, and he said it was a tie between The Swamp on *M*A*S*H* (not really a bar; just the still in Hawkeye's tent) and The Bronze on *Buffy the Vampire Slayer.* "The Bronze was a strange place. Teenagers hung out there, but drinks were served. They had interesting bands playing." And the bar had vampires -- which not every bar has. As for favorite TV church or clergyman, he went back to *M*A*S*H.* "Father Mulcahy was great."

A recurring theme throughout the year at bars and churches was the search for community. More and more, people seem to be finding community online; even through podcasts (which Tim called "radio without the listeners"). Still, the meetup at The 21st Amendment reminded us that hanging out with people is still important.

We weren't the only ones asking questions, though. When I told Kristen about our adventures over the year, she looked puzzled. "I understand about the bars," she said, "But why the churches?"

We were pretty sure nobody in, say, Alabama would have asked that question. We were definitely back home.

***

The next day, December 20, we drove to Santa Rosa. My sister Lola had graciously invited us to stay with her until we figured out what came next.

It was time to watch our California TV show, but we didn't have to make that decision on our own. Of the twenty shows I'd put on the ballot at the podcast meetup (plus Kate from Rwanda's addition), *Arrested Development* was the overwhelming winner. It's a show about a family of greedy, immoral (but hilarious) Californians who never go to church. And though the characters drink a lot, they don't seem to go to bars. We watched an episode the next day.

There was never any question what movie theater we'd visit on our return to California. The summer after graduating from high school, I got a job at the UA 6 Theater on 3rd Street in Santa Rosa. It was one of my best jobs ever; not only did I get to watch movies free (at any theater in town), but by bringing my own cup and bowl, I could have all the soda and popcorn I wanted. My brother worked next door at the video arcade above an ice cream parlor, so video games were free as well. (The only downside was having to pay for ice cream.)

The movie theater was still there, though it's under different ownership. We went to see *The Edge of Seventeen*, a coming of age film that was well reviewed but not very good. Sadly, the ice cream parlor and the video game arcade are long gone.

Choosing our California film had been an easy, early decision as well.

With our kids, we had a tradition of watching Christmas films on Christmas Eve Eve (the night before the night before Christmas). Once they were old enough for it, *Die Hard*, set and filmed in California, formed part of the rotation. We went to our son Bret's apartment to watch it with him.

We checked almost all our boxes for state 50: bar, movie theater, TV show, state movie. The only thing left to complete the project was going to church.

Before the trip began, I'd been pretty sure which church we'd be attending on Sunday, December 25, 2016.

***

An old showbiz adage -- where being upstaged was always a worry -- was "Don't work with children or animals." God doesn't seem to be concerned about it, and both kids and critters were in abundance at the early Christmas Eve service at First Presbyterian Church of Santa Rosa. My parents began attending this church when they moved from Los Angeles to Santa Rosa, not long before I was born; it's where I was baptized as a baby and where I went to church until I was about ten. Though my parents attended another church for years, they came back to First Presbyterian in their final years. Both my mom's and my dad's memorial services were held there. Even when our family attended other churches, we often went to the 11:00 pm Christmas Eve service.

This year, we'd decided to attend the 5:00 service, which had more families and young children in attendance. As Pastor Dale Flowers said in his welcome, "Kids, tonight's service is a little different. If your parents want to make noise or want to move around, that's okay. This is a night they can do those things."

There were plenty of children in attendance, many participating in various parts of the service. As we arrived about half an hour before the service was due to start, one little boy ran shouting into the building ahead of his parents, "Guys! Guys! I'm going into the church!" While we waited for the service to begin, costumed kids were running about, under adult supervision but just a little wildly.

The children were in costume for a paraphrased version of the Christmas story. When the little boy playing Joseph heard from an angel, he used a most excellent Macaulay Culkin/*Home Alone* expression of surprise, complete with wide eyes and hands on cheeks. Later, he pulled Mary to Bethlehem in a Radio Flyer wagon.

Some of the children in the stable were dressed as animals, while others wore cowboy hats, vests, and chaps (no explanation was given). Another kid dressed as a star led the Magi to the manger. They brought gifts of stuffed animals and a toy truck to the Baby Jesus. In other words, not everything came exactly from the Biblical text, but we enjoyed all of it.

As Brenna Hesch, the church's associate pastor, came forward to give the message, she said, "After that, I don't know if I need to say more…" Even when pastors say things like that, they always say more -- which was fine this time, because Brenna gave a good homily. She talked about the refugee crisis in Europe and how serious problems like that are easily replaced in her mind by "wedding planning, a new job, and *Rogue One*." She went on to draw parallels between the refugees and the shepherds of Luke 2.

After the service everyone went outside for hot chocolate and cookies next to a manger scene with a cow, some chickens, sheep, and a lamb less than a week old.

Honestly, we went to this Christmas Eve service at First Presbyterian for the same reason a lot of people go to church: family and friends would be there. We hoped to see my sister, her husband, their grown kids and some of the grandkids, and we were able to sit in the same row with a niece and nephew and to meet their newborn daughter. We hadn't been in the building long when I saw Diane, a friend since before we started school together.

That evening reminded us why people go to the same church -- or the same bar -- year after year. There's something special about being with people who know your whole story.

***

We wanted to attend the Christmas Eve service at another of our home churches as well, so we drove fifteen minutes north to Healdsburg Community Church, where we'd worshiped on our last Sunday in California at the end of 2015. Here, too, we knew we were among family.

The next morning, just to check all the boxes on our 52 Sunday adventure, we went back to First Presbyterian. We had reached our goal of visiting at least one bar and one church in each of the United States during one calendar year.

We'd often wondered how we'd feel if we had to stop before we finished our mission. If the nasty sounds from the engine made in Connecticut had been from the transmission rather than the spark plugs; if one of us -- or one of our kids -- had gotten sick or seriously hurt; if we'd maxed all our credit cards; if we'd had our identity stolen...so many things could have gone wrong. If we'd come up short, would the trip have still been worth it?

Every time we talked about it, all year long, from New Year's Day until Christmas, we knew. From the first weekend when we met Kathleen in Las Vegas, through every week when we saw friends and family we hadn't seen for years or met new friends and family we hope to stay in touch with for years to come. We saw so many places that people put on bucket lists and experiences we hadn't even thought to wish for. So from our perspective, the trip was definitely worthwhile.

But it was more than just the experience of a lifetime. All year, we heard conversations in bars, in churches, in homes, and even in movie theaters about life in the United States during a chaotic and divided time. We hadn't expected to finish the year with a definitive report that would bring the whole country to faith, but we were surprised to find that we ended the year with a little more hope than we had when we began the trip.

In both bars and churches, we discovered that people aren't completely sealed off from each other in a faceless internet world. People still gather as communities, seek comfort and comfort others. We were impressed by the way several bars provided a community for the lonely and outcasts and even looked for ways to meet people's material needs. We also saw churches that were incredibly creative in the ways they clothed the naked, fed the hungry, brought healing to the sick, and shared the Good News with the downcast.

Some people think only old people in the rural Bible Belt go to church these days, but big cities in blue states had some of the most vibrant churches we saw, where young people were singing and speaking the Gospel in new ways.

Jesus said He would build His church and the gates of Hell would not prevail against it. With our own eyes and ears, we learned that in the United States, at least, Jesus is still proclaimed for the many who are listening -- some of them in bars.

ACKNOWLEDGEMENTS

Most books' acknowledgments express gratitude to five or six or a dozen people. We, on the other hand, can't mention everyone who made this book possible without making this segment longer than the rest of the book.

This trip was possible because people invited us into their homes, welcomed us to their bars, and shared their ministries with us. Even before the trip began, a dozen or so people allowed us to store our belongings in their garages and storage sheds (or, in the case of the cat, in their homes). People have been praying for us since before the trip began, and some are still praying for us. Some friends and family (and one church) even provided financial support.

So to the best of our ability, we've listed the folks who, state by state, made our adventure possible. Without you, we would have had to stay home. Thank you.

January
Nevada: Kathleen, Tracy and Troy
Arizona: Clyde and Ann, Chuck and Janet, Larry and Linda, Uncle Paul and Brenda, Aunt Lola
New Mexico: Mary, Liz and Bill, David and Melanie, Robin
Texas: Julie and Dan, Bud, Chase, Bruce (though we didn't meet him) and Maryanne, Tiny, Z
Oklahoma: Jerry and Cordy, Alan, Tom and Lyn, Robert, David, Katie, John.

February
Kansas: Kevin and Marilyn

Missouri: Kathi and Matt, Jon and Briana, Amber and Phil, Saffron, Penelope, Imogen, Matt (thanks for the church recommendation!)

Arkansas: Phil and Tasha, Calum, Alena, Keely, and the Fort Smith Public Library (first of many libraries where we found shelter, comfort, and good Wifi)

Louisiana: Tom and Sonja, Adam and Megan, Lauren, Chris and Chris, Holly

March

Mississippi: John and Melanie, Corbin and Claire, Rick and Lynn, Lynn and Bob, JP

Alabama: Norman and Jackie, Conrad

Florida: John and Bonnie, Cathy, Uncle Paul, Jane and John, Betty and Mike, Andrew and Debra

Georgia: Jerry and Keiko, Tamami, Aiden

April

South Carolina: Kathi and John, Elizabeth

North Carolina: Robert and Kim, Robert and Samm, Phil, Patsy, Lucky and Li'l Santa

Tennessee: Craig and Beckie, Gretchen and Ray, Willa

Kentucky: Edie, Patty

May

West Virginia: Danita and JaRon

Virginia: Rob and Linda, Matthew and Kristen, James, Knox

Washington, D.C: Rachel, Jessica, Katie, Lennelle

Maryland: Claudia and Shimon, Isaac (and Emir, Rainn, and Tiangao), Ben

Delaware: Dave and Cari, Mark and Susan

June
Pennsylvania: Dan and Kathie, Chris, Rylan, Hannah
New Jersey: Allan and Fiona, Diana and Damian, Allie, Zoe, Ethan, Alice
New York: Joanne, Jil
Alaska: Stephen and Stacie, Jim and Kathy

July
Hawaii: Steve and Patricia, Adam and Wendy, Millie and Mason, Becky, Bethany, Charlie and Ingrid
Washington: Katie and Tony, Sami, Michael, Terry and Gail, Paige and Grant
Connecticut: Carrie, Erin, Chris and Katrina, Sydney, Olivia, Pete, the gang at Harp and Hound who recommended Ocean Mist
Rhode Island: Val and Alice, Lucy, Jim
Massachusetts: Paul, Jayne, Joanna and Alex, Sammy and Luke, Nick, Eric

August
New Hampshire: Cathy and Chip (thanks, Ziggy!), Bailey
Maine: Kate and Simon
Vermont: Dennis and Laurie, Jeff and Bethany, Michael and Jaye, and everybody at Living Hope Wesleyan
Ohio: David and Kelly, Kyra, David and Betty.

September
Michigan: Jonathan, Walid and Summer, Dwight and Jeanne

Indiana: Laura and Brad, Lizzie, Kriss and Andrew, Katie, Daniel, Amy, Grace, Jennifer and Mike, Nathan, Mom and Dad Date

Illinois: Brad and Rebecca, Lucie, Anna, Lara, Mike, Steve and Cindy, Eric, Deanna, Aunt Marilyn, Sue and Mike, Hannah and Chris, Sarah and Damon

Wisconsin: Craig, Penny

October

Minnesota: Daryl and Carol, Anna and Dan, Kelli, Carter, Colin, Maya, Tucker, Troy, Rick and Sue

Iowa: David and Connie, David and Beckie, Stephen and Florence, Josh

Nebraska: Tom and Paula, Shirley, staff of Eugene T. Mahoney State Park (and the Boy Scouts of America)

South Dakota: Bill and Jerri, Jake, Melody, Lia

North Dakota: Corinna and Geoff, Josh, Violet, Courtney, Father Odo, Rodney and Teri

November

Colorado: Dave and Becca, Kristie (we missed you, Jeremy)

Utah: Lisa and Jon, Pat and Judy

Wyoming: Jace and Hannah, Morgan, the Backwards family

December

Montana: Megan and Brian, Dawson, Kelby, David and Misty

Idaho: Clint and Bonnie, Anaka, Christina and Tom, Denny and Sharon, Brad, Janet and Warren, Joel, John and Marg

Oregon: Carol and Jim (we missed seeing you, Jim), John, Blake, Leonard, Jan and Fran, Esther, Kristina, Hannah, Rick and Maria,

Robin, Dale (Tag) and Nancy, Anne

California people helped us in all kinds of ways, like storing our stuff:
Bret, Dave and Lola, Jared and Jenna, Tim and Popie, Robert and
Carol, Mike and Kristie, Robert and Marsha, Archie and Sue, Sara, Jay
and Tracy (Zooey says hi!), Ken and Michelle, Susan and Caroline,
Todd and Heather.

Jason and Tim, thanks for everything.

Thanks especially to everybody who read the blogs (and told others
about it) and to those who read the first edition, where they got no
credit at all, even though they deserved a lot.

All the Bars We Walked into During 2016

Alabama The Collins Bar (where Dean made a bartender miserable), Birmingham

Alaska Mecca Bar (where Mindy was shocked by a drink's name), Fairbanks

Arizona The Shelter (which didn't have pinball), Tucson

Arkansas Rooster's on the Avenue (where the bouncer was friendly), Fort Smith

California 21st Amendment (where we met a bunch of people), San Francisco

Colorado The Principal's Office (which is, of course, in an old school building), Colorado Springs

Connecticut The Harp and the Hound (where patrons recommended a bar in Rhode Island), Mystic

Delaware Hutch's Pub (which takes pool seriously), Newark

Florida Mickey Quinn's Irish Pub (on Saint Patrick's Day!), Seminole

Georgia Joystick Gamebar (possibly Dean's favorite), Atlanta

Hawaii Sam's Oceanfront Restaurant and Bar (on the beach at sunset), Kapa'a

Idaho Pengilly's Saloon (where Mindy got an undeserved free cider), Boise

Illinois Cherry Street Restaurant and Bar (for sentimental reasons), Galesburg

Indiana Harry's Chocolate Shop (which had no chocolate at all), West Lafayette

Iowa The Blazing Saddle (which was the only busy bar around), Des Moines

Kansas The Cattlemen's Lounge (where we felt like members of the club), Dodge City

Kentucky The Wrigley Taproom and Eatery (which is designed for community), Corbin

Louisiana Buffa's (on the edge of the French Quarter), New Orleans

Maine The Drouthy Bear Pub (where we met some men on a quest), Camden

Maryland Hank Dietle's Tavern (with liquor license #001 and live music), Rockville

Massachusetts Liberty Tavern (a cradle of liberty), Clinton

Michigan Glengarry Inn (because it was nearby), Wolverine Lake

Minnesota Donny Dirk's Zombie Den (possibly Mindy's favorite), Minneapolis

Mississippi QuarterDeck Bar (where the bartender made us a cucumber cocktail), Long Beach

Missouri The Tank Room and Westport Flea Market (at one, we were invited to church. At the other, we met an old friend), Kansas City

Montana Iron Horse Bar and Grill (which is not what we expected), Missoula

Nebraska Nite Owl (with a movie!), Omaha

Nevada Aureole in Mandalay Bay (when we were still shy), Las Vegas

New Hampshire 815 (but it was a secret), Manchester

New Jersey Darby Road Pub (which was quite crowded), Scotch Plains

New Mexico Maria's New Mexican Kitchen (where we enjoyed sopapillas), Santa Fe

New York Afternoones Restaurant and Bar (in which Dean got rebuffed), Staten Island

North Carolina Lazy Hiker Brewing Company (where Mindy actually enjoyed a beer), Franklin

North Dakota Hanson's (which may be the geographical center of

North America), Robinson

Ohio Slapsy Maxies and Level One, Columbus (plus Black Cloister, Toledo, where a church meets)

Oklahoma Ned's (which doesn't smell of smoke despite the reviews), Talequah

Oregon Porters (where we felt more welcome than we expected), Medford

Pennsylvania Paddy's Pub (which was nicer than on television), Philadelphia

Rhode Island Ocean Mist Beach Bar (where we also met horses), Matunuck

South Carolina McHale's Irish Pub (which serves the community), Rock Hill

South Dakota The Old Style Saloon #10 (legendary!), Deadwood

Tennessee Embers Ski Lodge (where Dean enjoyed a basketball game), Nashville

Texas The Barbershop (no haircutting, just dogs and children), Dripping Springs

Utah Brewvies (where we were glad to be over 21), Salt Lake City

Vermont Charlie-O's World Famous Bar and Fine Dining (which didn't serve food), Montpelier

Virginia Los Toltecos Authentic Mexican Bar and Grill (for Cinco de Mayo), Alexandria

Washington Three Lions Pub (where we know people gave us pseudonyms), Redmond

West Virginia Domestic (where the evening seemed to have begun several hours earlier), Shepherdstown

Wisconsin Tom's Old Bogies Bar (which our niece recommended), Holcombe

Wyoming Backwards Distilling Company (where Mindy had the most yummy hot chocolate), Casper

And **Washington D.C.** Church and States

All the churches we went to in 2016

Alabama 16th Street Baptist Church, Birmingham

Jimmy Hale Mission, Birmingham

Alaska University Baptist Church, Fairbanks

Fairbanks Seventh Day Adventist Church

Arizona Beth Sar Shalom, Tucson

Grace Community Church, Tucson

SIL Mexico Branch, Catalina

Arkansas First Presbyterian Church, Fort Smith

The Next Step Homeless Services, Fort Smith

California First Presbyterian Church of Santa Rosa

Healdsburg Community Church

Colorado Scum of the Earth, Denver

Monument Community Presbyterian Church, Monument

Connecticut Hope Evangelical Free Church, Wilton

First Church of Christ, Wethersfield

Delaware Newark Church of Christ

The Journey, Newark

Florida First Baptist Church Indian Rocks, Largo

Georgia Clairmont Presbyterian Church, Decatur

Shallowford Presbyterian Church, Atlanta

Renovation Church, Atlanta

Hawaii Kauai Christian Fellowship South, Kilauea

Idaho Sanctuary Cowboy Church, Middleton

All Saints Presbyterian Church, Boise

Illinois Geneseo Evangelical Free Church

Indiana Covenant Church, West Lafayette

Southport Presbyterian, Indianapolis

Iowa Alive Church, Des Moines

Valley Church, Des Moines

Kansas Whitestone Mennonite Church, Hesston

Kentucky Morris Fork Presbyterian Church

Louisiana Vieux Carre Baptist Church, New Orleans

Maine The Rock, Bangor

Hancock Point Chapel

Maryland Our Lady of Mercy Church, Rockville

Rockville Assembly of God

Massachusetts Trinity Congregational Church, Bolton

Michigan Arabic Evangelical Alliance, Madison Heights

NorthRidge Church, Plymouth

Arab American Friendship Center, Detroit

Minnesota Hope Community Church, Minneapolis

Global Fingerprints, Evangelical Free Church of America, Minneapolis

Mississippi First Baptist Church, Long Beach

Missouri Forerunner Christian Fellowship, Grandview

Redeemer Fellowship, Kansas City

Montana Dillon Assembly of God

Nebraska Boy Scout Jubilee Protestant worship service, Mahoney State Park

Holy Family Shrine, Gretna

The Rock (college worship service) Candlewood Church, Omaha

Candlewood Church, Lincoln

Nevada First Christian Church (Disciples of Christ) Las Vegas

Las Vegas Rescue Mission family worship

New Hampshire Pilgrim Pines Camp, Swanzey

New Jersey Terrill Road Bible Chapel, Fanwood

New Mexico Eldorado Community Church, Santa Fe

New York Salem Church, Staten Island

North Carolina First Baptist Church, Franklin

North Dakota Assumption Abbey, Richardton

Sims-Almont Lutheran Church, Almont

Ohio Threshold Church, Toledo

Mosaic Ministries, Toledo

Oklahoma Elm Tree Baptist Church, Tahlequah

Oregon Capernaum (Young Life) Portland

Bear Creek Church, Medford

Pennsylvania Harbor Light Chapel, Harrisburg

Rhode Island Perryville Bible Church

South Carolina St. John United Methodist Church, Fort Mill

South Dakota The Filling Station, Sturgis

Hills of Grace Fellowship, Rapid City

Tennessee Midtown Fellowship, 12 South, Nashville

Texas Reach Church, Austin

Saint Catherine of Siena Catholic Church, Austin

Utah Jordan Valley (formerly Jordan Presbyterian) Church, West Jordan

Saint Vincent de Paul Dining Hall, Salt Lake City

Vermont Living Hope Wesleyan Church, Waterbury Center

Virginia Tree of Life Ministries, Purcellville

St. Matthews Church, Sterling

Washington Redmond Presbyterian Church

West Virginia Fellowship Bible Church, Shenandoah Junction

Warrior Creek Development, McDowell County

Wisconsin Saint Francis of Assisi Roman Catholic, Flambeau

First Church of Christ, Ladysmith

Abundant Life Assembly of God, Ladysmith

Wyoming Cornerstone Evangelical Free Church, Casper

College Heights Baptist Church, Casper

St. Mark's Episcopal Church, Casper

And **Washington D.C.** Capitol Hill Baptist Church

The Table

Washington National Cathedral

Washington DC CSM

All the movie theaters and the movies in 2016

In our quest to see movies in theaters in every state this year (plus one in the nation's capital), we sometimes had to go to a bad movie or a bad theater in order to see a movie that week. And that's okay. In other words, these aren't endorsements, just lists.

Alabama, Wynnsong Cinemas, Mobile *Zootopia*

Alaska, The Blue Loon, Fairbanks *The Meddler*

Arizona, The Loft, Tucson *Hitchcock/Truffaut*

Arkansas, Malco Theater, Fort Smith *Lady in the Van*

California, 3rd Street Cinema, Santa Rosa *The Edge of Seventeen*

Colorado, Chapel Hills 13 Cinema, Monument *Hacksaw Ridge*

Connecticut, Luxury Cinemas, Mystic *Hunt for the Wilderpeople*

Delaware, Cinemark in Christiana Mall, Newark *The Nice Guys*

Florida, Tree House Theater, Gulf Breeze *Anomalisa*

Georgia, Regal Cinema, Savannah *Miracles from Heaven*

Hawaii, Kukui Grove Theater, Lihue *Central Intelligence*

Idaho, Northgate Reel Theater, Boise *The Magnificent Seven*

Illinois, AMC Theater, Naperville *Don't Think Twice*

Indiana, Tibbs Drive-in, Indianapolis *9 Lives, Pete's Dragon, The Secret Lives of Pets*

Cinemark Movies 8, Greenwood, *Kubo and the Two Strings*

Iowa, Fleur Cinema and Cafe, Des Moines *The Queen of Katwe*

Kansas, Plaza Cinema, Ottawa *Kung Fu Panda III*

Kentucky, Movie Palace, Elizabethville *The Jungle Book*

Louisiana, Theaters at Canal Place, New Orleans *The Maltese Falcon*

Maine, Eveningstar Theater, Brunswick *Cafe Society*

Maryland, The Senator Theater, Baltimore *The Family Fang*

Massachusetts, Imax at Jordan's Furniture, Reading *Star Trek Beyond*

Michigan, Regal Cinemas, Novi *The Insanity of God*

Minnesota, AMC Theater, Edina *Sully*

Mississippi, Cinemark Theater, Pearl *Race*

Missouri, Cinemark in the Plaza, Kansas City *Hail Caesar*

Montana, The Roxy Theater, Missoula *Moonlight*

          Big Sky Cinema, Dillon, *Moana* (we didn't post about it, though)

Nebraska, Village Pointe Theater, Omaha *Miss Peregrine's School for Peculiar Children*

Nevada, Brenden Theaters and Imax at the Palms, Las Vegas *The Big Short*

New Hampshire, Gilford Cinema 8, Gilford *Ghostbusters*

New Jersey, The Princeton Garden Theater *The Man Who Knew Infinity*

New Mexico, Icon Theater, Albuquerque *Sisters*

New York, United Artists Theater, Staten Island *Ali*

North Carolina, Ruby Cinemas, Franklin *God's Not Dead II*

North Dakota, Grand 22, Bismarck *I'm Not Ashamed*

Ohio, Gateway Film Center, Columbus *Hell or High Water*

Oklahoma, AMC at Quail Springs Mall, Oklahoma City *The Good Dinosaur*

Oregon, Living Room Theater, Portland *Loving*

Pennsylvania, Colonial Theater, Phoenixville *Carrie*

Rhode Island, Misquamicut Drive-in, Misquamicut *Forrest Gump*

South Carolina, Regal Cinema, Atlanta *Risen*

South Dakota, The Historic Elks Theater, Rapid City *Priceless*

Tennessee, Regal Cinemas, Nashville *Love and Friendship* (at the Nashville Film Festival!)

Texas, North Park Alamo Drafthouse, San Antonio *The Revenant*

Utah, Brewvies, Salt Lake City *Doctor Strange*

Vermont, The Savoy, Montpelier *Captain Fantastic*

Virginia, Regal Cinemas, Glen Allen, *Captain America: Civil War*

Washington, Regal Cinemas, Redmond *Finding Dory*

West Virginia, The Park Palace, Charleston *My Name Is Doris*

Wisconsin, Miner Theater, Ladysmith *Hotel Transylvania II*

Wyoming, Studio City 11 at Mesa, Casper *Arrival*

Washington D. C., Landmark E Street Theater *Sing Street*

All the small-screen movies 0f 2016 (in the order we watched them)

In addition to watching a big-screen movie at a theater in every state, we also watched a movie on a small(ish) screen each week, but that movie had to be set or filmed in the state we were visiting. We travelled with a folder of DVDs that had something for most of the states, but not all, so sometimes we streamed the film -- or even found it on TCM at a motel.

1. Nevada - *Lost in America* (1985)
2. Arizona - *Raising Arizona* (1987)
3. New Mexico - *Silverado* (1985)
4. Texas - *Office Space* (1999)
5. Oklahoma - *Oklahoma* (1955)
6. Kansas - *Elmer Gantry* (1960)
7. Missouri - *Paper Moon* (1973)
8. Arkansas - *True Grit* (1969)
9. Louisiana - *Miller's Crossing* (1990)
10. Mississippi - *My Dog Skip* (2000)
11. Alabama - *My Cousin Vinny* (1992)
12. Florida - *Matinee* (1993)
13. Georgia - *The General* (1926)
14. South Carolina - *The Great Santini* (1979)
15. North Carolina - *Bull Durham* (1988)
16. Tennessee - *Starman* (1984)
17. Kentucky - *Goldfinger* (1964)
18. West Virginia - *A Killing Affair* (1977)
19. Virginia - *The Littlest Rebel* (1935)
20. Maryland - *Broadcast News* (1987)

21. Delaware - *Clean and Sober* (1988)

22. Pennsylvania - *Rocky* (1976)

23. New Jersey - *The Station Agent* (2003)

24. New York - *When Harry Met Sally* (1989)

25. Alaska - *The Gold Rush* (1925)

26. Hawaii - *Lilo and Stitch* (2002)

27. Washington - *House of Games* (1987)

28. Connecticut - *Beetlejuice* (1988)

29. Rhode Island - *Moonrise Kingdom* (2012)

30. Massachusetts - *The Crucible* (1996)

31. New Hampshire - *What About Bob?* (1991)

32. Maine - *The Iron Giant* (1999)

33. Vermont - *Nothing Sacred* (1937)

34. Ohio - *The Kings of Summer* (2013)

35. Michigan - *Grosse Pointe Blank* (1997)

36. Indiana - *Hoosiers* (1986)

37. Illinois - *The Untouchables* (1987)

38. Wisconsin - *Wayne's World* (1992)

39. Minnesota - *A Serious Man* (2009)

40. Iowa - *Field of Dreams* (1989)

41. Nebraska - *About Schmidt* (2002)

42. South Dakota - *North by Northwest* (1959)

43. North Dakota - *Fargo* (1996)

44. Colorado - *The Prestige* (2006)

45. Utah - *Fletch* (1985)

46. Wyoming - *Unforgiven* (1992)

47. Montana - *Little Big Man* (1970)

48. Idaho - *Napoleon Dynamite* (2004)

49. Oregon - *Meek's Cutoff* (2010)

50. California - *Die Hard* (1988)

Washington D.C.- *The Day the Earth Stood Still* (1951)

TV Shows for all 50 States (in the order we watched them)

For our own amusement, we watched television shows set or filmed in each of the states, using a variety of sources to find material. We found many of the shows on Youtube, but we also used Hulu, Amazon, Netflix, and whatever we could find on television wherever we were. We had a few DVDs as well. As was true with movies, some states have many shows to choose from, while other states... Well, we had to stretch the definition of "set and/or filmed in" a few times.

1) Nevada - *Crime Story* (1986)

2) Arizona - *Sky King* (1951)

3) New Mexico - *Better Call Saul* (2015)

4) Texas - *King of the Hill* (1997)

5) Oklahoma - *Carnivale* (2003)

6) Kansas - *Gunsmoke* (1955)

7) Missouri - *The John Larroquette Show* (1993)

8) Arkansas - *Evening Shade* (1990)

9) Louisiana - *Treme* (2010)

10) Mississippi - *In the Heat of the Night* (1988)

11) Alabama - *Hart of Dixie* (2011)

12) Florida - *Fresh Off the Boat* (2015)

13) Georgia - *The Walking Dead* (Season One - 2010)

14) South Carolina - *American Gothic* (1995)

15) North Carolina - The Andy Griffith Show (1960)

16) Tennessee - *Nashville* (2012)

17) Kentucky - *Justified* (2010)

18) West Virginia - *The X-Files* (1995 - episode 731)

19) Virginia - *The Waltons* (1971)

Bonus - Washington, D.C. - *Veep* (2012)

20) Maryland - *Homicide: Life on the Street* (1993)

21) Delaware - *The Pretender* (1996)

22) Pennsylvania - *It's Always Sunny in Philadelphia* (2005)

23) New Jersey - *The Sopranos* (1999)

24) New York - *Unbreakable Kimmy Schmidt* (2015)

25) Alaska - *Northern Exposure* (1990)

26) Hawaii - *Lost* (2004)

27) Washington - *Twin Peaks* (1990)

28) Connecticut - *Gilmore Girls* (2000)

29) Rhode Island - *Brotherhood* (2006)

30) Massachusetts - *Cheers* (1982)

31) New Hampshire - *The Path* (2016)

32) Maine - *Dark Shadows* (1966)

33) Vermont - *Newhart* (1982)

34) Ohio - *Fernwood 2night* (1977)

35) Michigan - *Battle Creek* (2015)

36) Indiana - *Parks and Recreation* (2009)

37) Illinois - *Kolchak: The Night Stalker* (1974)

38) Wisconsin - *Happy Days* (1974)

39) Minnesota - *The Mary Tyler Moore Show* (1970)

40) Iowa - *Drexell's Class* (1991)
         Double Trouble (1984)

41) Nebraska - *The Young Riders* (1989)

42) South Dakota - *Deadwood* (2004)

43) North Dakota - *Fargo* (2014)

44) Colorado - *Community* (2009)

45) Utah - *Big Love* (2006)

46) Wyoming - *Longmire* (2012)

47) Montana - *Buckskin* (1958)

48) Idaho - *The Grinder* (2015)

49) Oregon - *Portlandia* (2015)

50) California - *Arrested Development* (2003)

Tips for Sharing a Minivan for a Year without Killing Each Other
Pray a lot.

Packing Tips
Don't pack clothes like Dean. He did a little sorting of clothes while we were packing up (to be fair, he was busy doing a lot of other things, like working until the very end, writing almost all the blog posts, preaching, and figuring out how to fit everything we were taking into the van), but for the most part, he stuffed all the clothes in his closet and dresser drawers into a couple suitcases and four giant trash bags the morning we left California. In Nevada, he sorted through everything and got down to two suitcases plus his suit and winter gear.

Don't pack clothes like Mindy. She got rid of everything except two pairs of black jeans, assorted long and short sleeved T-shirts, and some dresses and sweaters. She went shopping every chance she got all year long, donating as she went, keeping two carry-on sized bags full of everyday clothes plus a black dress and winter gear. She never found a pair of cowboy boots she liked.

In addition to clothes, we had two laundry hampers full of camping gear (everything from the tent and sleeping bags to matches and a tea kettle), a box of books for reading and giving away, a container of food for snacking in the car and making light meals (peanut butter, honey, popcorn, chocolate chips -- the necessities of life), a box of things for giving away, Mindy's big box-o-crafts, tire chains, a box of dvd and cd binders (including state TV shows, state movies, and the road trip mix tapes that our kids had made for Mindy's Christmas gift), a pack of important documents (tax paperwork, birth certificates, insurance information and the like), and the very important computer bag.

All the Nights: motels, hotels, houses, tents, and the minivan

We aimed to stay in each state around a week, but some states (sorry, Alaska) got short-changed, while others (looking at you, Florida) got extensions. When we could, we tried to visit more than one part of a state. Here's where we stayed in each state (in chronological, not alphabetical, order)

January
Nevada
>Best Western McCarren Airport, Las Vegas (4 nights)

Arizona
>Phoenix Hostel and Cultural Center, Phoenix (1 night)
>Best Western, Phoenix (1 night)
>Setterlands' home, Tucson (3 nights)
>Snydals' home, Tucson (3 nights)

New Mexico
>Rodeway Inn, Albuquerque (1 night)
>Southalls' home, Santa Fe (3 nights)

Texas
>Best Western, Brownfield (1 night)
>Fiesta Best Western, San Antonio (2 nights)
>Poirers' home, Dripping Springs (4 nights)
>Motel 6, Canton (1 night)
>Snells' home (2 nights)

Oklahoma
>Blue Feather Bed and Breakfast, Tahlequah (4 nights)
>Comfort Inn and Suites, Oklahoma City (1 night)
>Krueckes' home, Midwest City (1 night)

February
Kansas
>Wyatt Earp Inn & Hotel, Dodge City (2 nights)
>Hesston College Guesthouse, Hesston (3 nights)
>Travelodge, Ottawa (1 night)

Missouri

    Best Western Riverside, Hannibal (2 nights)

    DeCanios' home, Grandview (5 nights)

Arkansas

    Best Western Eureka Inn, Eureka Springs (1 night)

    First Presbyterian guest house, Fort Smith (4 nights)

    Quality Inn and Suites, North Little Rock (1 night)

Louisiana

    Baymont Hotel, Shreveport (1 night)

    Days Inn, New Orleans airport (2 nights)

    Vieux Carre Baptist Church (3 nights)

March

Mississippi

    Days Inn, McComb (1 night)

    Columbus Inn, Columbus (1 night)

    Sheplers' home, Long Beach (4 nights)

Alabama

    Motel in or near Mobile (1 night)

    Motel in or near Montgomery (1 night)

    Tannehill State Park, McCalla (2 nights tent, 3 nights cabin)

Florida

    Econolodge Inn and Suites, Pensacola (1 night)

    Ochlockonee River State Park, Sockchoppy (1 night)

    Nystroms' home, Seminole (6 nights)

    Suburban Extended Stay South, Orlando (1 night)

    Krals' home, Orlando (1 night)

Georgia

    Lillises' home, Atlanta (6 nights)

    Motel in Savannah (1 night)

April

South Carolina

    James Island County Park (1 night tent)

Hotel near Columbia (1 night)

North Carolina

Riebes' home, just over the border in Charleston (4 nights)

Econo Lodge, Salisbury (1 night)

Motel near Glen Alpine (1 night)

Knights Inn, Franklin (4 nights)

Tennessee

Hotel in Knoxville (2 nights)

Snows' home, Nashville (5 nights)

Kentucky

Super 8 Motel, Munfordville (1 night)

Cumberland Falls State Resort Park, Corbin (tent, 2 nights)

Morris Fork Church, Morris Fork (4 nights)

Comfort Inn, Lexington (1 night)

West Virginia

Snows' home, Big Creek (1 night)

Hotel near Wheeling (1 night)

Pullers' home, Harper's Ferry (3 nights)

May

Virginia

Sleep Inn and Suites, Harrisonburg (1 night)

Andersons' home, Boone (2 night)

Merolas' home, Sterling (5 nights)

Quality Inn, Tyson's Corner (2 nights)

Washington D.C.

Douglas Memorial Methodist Church CSM office (3 nights)

Maryland

Super 8, Jessup (2 nights)

Liangs' home, Rockville (4 nights)

Econolodge Oceanfront, Ocean City (1 night)

Delaware

Sonesta Extended Stay, Newark (3 nights)

Newark Church of Christ parking lot, Newark (1 night)

Delaware House Travel Plaza, Newark (1 night)

Rodeway Inn University, Newark (1 night)

Pennsylvania

Hotel outside Lancaster (1 night)

Hotel near Phoenixville (2 nights)

Zipfs' friends in Hershey (1 night)

All-American Travel Plaza, Frystown (1 night)

Wilco Travel Plaza, Harrisburg (1 night)

Hotel near Harrisburg (1 night)

June

New Jersey

Hotel near Princeton (1 night)

Hotel near Asbury Park (1 night)

Wilks' home, Scotch Plain (4 nights)

New York

Hotel near Woodstock (1 night)

Hotel on Long Island (1 night? Maybe 2)

Blums' home, Staten Island (4 nights)

Connecticut

Porters' home, Rowayton (2 nights)

New York

Hotel near JFK (1 night)

Washington

Hotel near SeaTac (1 night)

Alaska

Ishams' home, Fairbanks (4 nights)

Washington

Hotel near SeaTac (1 night)

July

Hawaii

Airbnb, Kapa'a (tent, 7 nights)

Washington

Lowes' home, Redmond (4 nights)

Connecticut

Porters' home, Rowayton (2 nights)

Hadnots' home, Gale's Ferry (1 night)

TA Truck Service, Marion (1 night)

Porters' home, Rowayton (2 nights)

Rhode Island

Burlingame State Park, Charlestown (tent, 5 nights)

Massachusetts

Bennetts' home, North Atterbury (3 nights)

Langbergs' home, Lancaster (4 nights)

August

New Hampshire

New Hampshire Welcome Center, Seabrook (1 night)

New Hampshire Welcome Center, Hooksett -- northbound and southbound (2 nights)

Chesleys' family home, Hopkinton (1 night)

Pilgrim Pines Camp and Conference Center, Swanzey (tent, 3 nights)

Maine

Kennebunk Service Area (1 night)

Paul Bunyan Campground, Bangor (tent, 4 nights)

The House of Relentless Creativity (1 night)

Walmart, Lamoine (1 night)

Vermont

Super Sparkle Laundry, Barre (1 night)

EconoLodge, Montpelier (1 night)

Parking lot behind a business, Waterbury (1 night)

Little River State Park, Waterbury (tent, 1 night)

Dennis' home, Richmond (3 nights)

New York

Warners Travel Plaza, Warners (1 night)

Anchor Motel, Niagara Falls (1 night)

Ohio

Kaisers' home, Maumee (4 nights)

EconoLodge, Worthington (2 nights)

September

Michigan

Andersons' home, Wolverine Lake (6 nights)

Indiana

Bowes' home, Indianapolis (1 night)

Greenwood Village South guest room, Greenwood (1 night)

Rees' home, Ladoga (1 night)

Woodards' home, West Lafayette (5 nights)

Illinois

Gundlachs' home, Lindenhurst (1 night)

Bekermeiers' home, Palatine (1 night)

Palms' home, Geneseo (4 nights)

Greys' home, Rockford (1 night)

Wisconsin

Andersons' vacation home, Holcombe Lake (5 nights)

October

Minnesota

    Andersons' home, Lakeville (9 nights)

Iowa

    Walmart, Indianola (1 night)

    Dr Davids' home, Clive (4 nights)

Nebraska

    Walmart, Omaha (1 night)

    Econo Lodge, Omaha (2 nights)

    Mahoney State Park, Ashland (3 nights)

    Econo Lodge, Kearney (1 night)

South Dakota

    Main Stay Suites, Rapid City (1 night)

    Franklin Historic Hotel, Deadwood (1 night)

    Walmart, Rapid City (1 night)

    Econo Lodge, Rapid City (3 nights)

North Dakota

    Walmart, Mandan (1 night)

    Sunflower Inn, Almont (5 nights)

Minnesota

    Andersons' home, Lakeville (1 night)

November

Indiana

    Woodards' home, West Lafayette (1 night)

    Greenwood Village South guest room, Greenwood (5 nights)

Missouri

    Suburban Extended Stay, Columbia (1 night)

Kansas

    Sleep Inn and Suites, Salina (1 night)

Colorado

      Jordan-Irwins' home, Monument (7 nights)

Utah

      Quality Inn, Vernal (1 night)

      Webers' home, Sandy (2 nights)

      Sleep Inn, Sandy (2 nights)

Wyoming

      The Royal Inn, Casper (7 nights)

December

Montana

      Econo Lodge, Billings (1 night)

      Paces' home, Hamilton (2 nights)

      Sleep Inn, Missoula (1 night)

      Sunset Motel, Dillon (3 nights)

Idaho

      Lutzs' home, Twin Falls (2 nights)

      Mintuns' home, Boise (1 night)

      Wilmorths' home, Boise (2 nights)

      Erismans' home, Boise (2 nights)

Oregon

      Sleep Inn, Ontario (1 night)

      Pfeils' home, Bend (1 night)

      Comfort Inn, Portland (2 nights)

      Meadors' friends' home, Medford (3 nights)

California

      Thunderbird Lodge, Redding (1 night)

      Rodeway, Rohnert Park (1 night)

      Johnsons' home (7 nights)

      Bret's home (2 nights)

ABOUT THE AUTHORS

Dean and Mindy were born in different states; he in California and she in Ohio. Dean graduated from San Diego State University. Mindy graduated from Taylor University in Upland, Indiana. They met at Trinity Evangelical Divinity School in Deerfield, Illinois.

Mindy lived next door to a church for most of her childhood, and she planned to be a missionary when she grew up. Dean worked at churches as an intern, a youth pastor, an interim, and a "director of arts in worship."

For years, Dean worked next to bartenders in hotels. Mindy is pretty sure she never ordered alcohol in a bar before our trip began.

Dean wrote the nine Bill the Warthog mystery books for children; Mindy worked for three different newspapers, but loves editing as much as writing.

Dean and Mindy celebrated their 30th wedding anniversary and their 55rh birthdays in 2016. They're still married, and they're still visiting churches and bars (and watching movies). The minivan is still their only vehicle.

CPSIA information can be obtained
at www.ICGtesting.com
Printed in the USA
FSHW01n2047190618
49616FS